Legal Guide To Buying And Selling Art And Collectibles

Armen R. Vartian, Esq.

Bonus Books, Inc., Chicago

© 1997 by Armen R. Vartian, Esq.
All rights reserved.

01 00 99 98 97   5 4 3 2 1

Library of Congress Cataloging-in-Publication Data

Vartian, Armen R.
    Legal guide to buying and selling art and collectibles / Armen R. Vartian.
        p.   cm.
    Includes index.
    ISBN 1-56625-079-X (pbk.)
    1. Law and art—United States—Popular works.   I. Title.
KF4288.Z9V37   1997
344.73'097—dc21   96-51959

Bonus Books, Inc., 160 East Illinois Street, Chicago, Illinois 60611

On the cover:

Balinese Girl (1932) by Nicolai Fechin (1881–1955) courtesy of Fechin Art Reproductions, P.O. Box 220, San Cristobal, NM 87564. Photo by Pat Pollard.

1913 nickel (one of four known and worth over $1 million) courtesy of Professional Coin Grading Service, P.O. Box 9458, Newport Beach, CA 92658. Photo by Jon Bahner.

1952 Topps Mickey Mantle "rookie" card (the most sought-after modern sports card) courtesy of Professional Sports Authenticators, P.O. Box 6180, Newport Beach, CA 92658. Photo by Jon Bahner.

2¢ Hawaii missionary stamp (Scott 1; one of 15 known, it was sold in September 1996 for $200,000) courtesy of Shreve's Philatelic Galleries, 14131 Midway Road, Dallas, TX 75244.

Sun Records "Good Rockin' Tonight" by Elvis Presley courtesy of Good Rockin' Tonight, 700 East Alton, Santa Ana, CA 92705

Printed in the United States of America

Contents

Introduction

Buying art and collectibles is a passion for Americans. From the imposing sales rooms at Sotheby's to the local swap meet, we search for objects that are interesting or which will increase in value over time (hopefully, both). Billions of dollars are spent every year, and the numbers are increasing. But few of us know where to go to learn our legal rights and remedies when buying or selling art and collectibles. For example, what if a work of art turns out to be a fake? Or a "rare" stamp or coin isn't as rare as the dealer said? When buying or selling through auction houses, can you negotiate the commission and other terms? Are insurance and other expenses related to art or collectibles tax deductible? This book answers those questions and many, many others, and gives the reader a good working knowledge of legal aspects of buying and selling art and collectibles.

The book is divided into four parts. Part One relates to buying and selling art or collectible items through retail galleries or shops, including getting good title, warranties of grade and authenticity, and buying for investment. Part Two relates to buying and selling at public auction, including contractual provisions in auction contracts and the mechanics of bidding at auction. Part Three covers resolution of disputes involving art and collectibles, from negotiating with dealers to suing in court. And Part Four discusses the tax aspects of buying and selling art and collectibles, including sales and use tax, deductibility of insurance and other expenses, charitable donations of art and collectibles, and other issues.

I hope you will find this book useful not only for problems you may have right now, but also as a general reference throughout your collecting life. But be warned: Individual situations differ, and no single book can substitute for the advice of a competent attorney on a specific point. This book is not intended as your *only* source for legal information. Nor do I expect to make lawyers out of each of you. Think of this book as your *first* source. If you have a problem, read my general discussion here. Then, when you consult an attorney, you'll know how to describe the problem and what specific questions you'll need answered. And happy collecting!

Part One:
Buying and Selling Art and
Collectibles through Dealers

What happens if the Sung vase, Matisse print, or Jimi Hendrix guitar you bought a few months (or years) back turns out to be a fake? Or the uncirculated coin you bought turns out to be circulated? Is the dealer responsible? Whether there is a 10-page written agreement, or simply a handshake, the purchase of art or collectible items always constitutes a contract between buyer and seller. Chapter 1 explains what is commonly found in that contract and why written contracts are so important, and Chapter 2 explains how key warranties and disclaimers allocate the risks of buying such items between buyers and sellers.

1

The Written Contract

I always advise clients to "get it in writing." This is good advice generally when you are buying anything on the basis of what a salesman tells you. But it is especially important when buying art or collectibles, for reasons we will see throughout this chapter.

The Statute of Frauds

The most important reason for a written contract is a practical one. The parties to an agreement should have something besides their own memories to rely upon in remembering the terms of that agreement. Even close friends know that agreements are stronger and more closely followed if they are in writing and unambiguous. But there is also a good legal reason to have a written agreement. Oral agreements to sell art or collectibles may not be enforceable against the dealer, based on a very old principle of law called the Statute of Frauds. The Statute of Frauds, which is incorporated in most states' laws through Section 2-201 of the Uniform Commercial Code (UCC), declares that contracts for the sale of goods over $500 are not enforceable unless they are in writing and signed by the party to be charged with the obligation. The purpose of this rule is to avoid "your word against mine" litigation over exactly what oral agreements might have been made between buyers and sellers. The document need not be formal. In fact, the official comment to UCC §2-201 states that "It may be written in lead pencil on a scratch pad." The writing requirements, as summarized in the UCC, are as follows:

> First, it must evidence a contract for the sale of goods; second, it must be "signed," a word which includes any authentication which identifies the party to be charged; and third, it must specify a quantity.

Contract = Offer + Acceptance

Taking these individually, UCC §2-201 requires that the writing "evidence a contract for the sale of goods," as opposed to an offer to negotiate a sale, or an offer to do something else. For example, consider a letter signed by John Smith stating, "I'd like to sell you my Mickey Mantle rookie card for $75,000. Write me if you are interested." This is not a contract, but merely an offer. The recipient must *accept* the offer, by writing back something to the effect of "I accept your offer to buy your Mantle card for $75,000," or even "I accept the offer in your recent letter to me." Without an acceptance, Mr. Smith could withdraw the offer at any time and sell the card to someone else. But an offer letter and acceptance letter, taken together, would constitute a writing satisfying the UCC, and both parties would be legally bound to complete the transaction.

Likewise, if Mr. Smith had written that "I'd be willing to let you have my Mantle card for six months for $1,000," that could not be interpreted as a contract of sale, because Mr. Smith isn't offering to pass title to the card. Rather, he is offering to loan it for a fixed period of time for a price which is far less than the card's market value. If the recipient wrote back accepting the offer, he could not expect that he would end up owning the card because there was no writing evidencing a sale.

The Signature Requirement—Who's Doing Business with Whom?

The second §2-201 requirement is that the writing must be "signed," through some "authentication which identifies the party to be charged." There doesn't have to be an original signature, and in most commercial contracts neither party actually *signs* the written documents. However, the use of a dealer's invoice form, handwritten identification of the parties, or anything else clearly stating who is doing business with whom will satisfy the UCC.

The "signing" requirement raises two other important points: (1) know exactly whom you're dealing with; (2) try to have the other guy draw up at least part of the agreement. Beyond stating the obvious, identifying the other party to the contract can be very important where the parties might be doing business either personally or through a corporation. I once represented a man who had a claim against an art gallery owned by Ms. X. My client always believed that the gallery owner was personally responsible for the debt because his contract was with "X Gallery," and Ms. X signed the contract. Ms. X, on the other hand, said her gallery was operated by a corporation whose name did not even resemble "X Gallery." Needless to say, by the time the case reached court, the corporation had no assets, and Ms. X refused to pay out of her own pocket. Proper identification of the parties would have solved the problem one way or another. Either Ms. X would have bound herself personally to the deal, or my client would have been told that he was dealing with a corporation, and he might have thought twice about it.

In addition, having at least part of the contract documents prepared on the other party's forms or stationery will help avoid a situation where the party denies having entered into the contract.

Must Include Quantity—Don't Have to Include Price

The third §2-201 requirement is that the contract state a "quantity." With art and collectible items this is not a big issue, although it could be for the sale of bulk items such as silver bullion coins or sheets of postage stamps. Note that the UCC does not require that the written documents contain the contract price. This seems odd, given the vital importance of price to any purchase or sale agreement. The UCC's attitude, however, is that the court can use market information to insert a reasonable price into a contract if the parties argue over what was agreed, but the court cannot tell the parties *how many* of a particular item should be sold.

Exceptions to the Statute of Frauds

Enforcing the Statute of Frauds is becoming less popular in the increasingly "paperless" business world of the 1990s. Over the years, the UCC has adopted certain "exceptions," *i.e.*, situations where the existence of the contract can be proven without a written memorandum. The most common such situation is when the contract has been acknowledged by the parties' performance, such as when the seller has accepted payment for the goods and the goods have been accepted by the buyer. So, for example, an art dealer cannot deny the contract of sale for a painting if he delivers the painting to the buyer and cashes the buyer's check. However, keep in mind that without a written agreement, anything *else* that may have been agreed orally by the dealer—such as a return privilege or warranties regarding provenance and attribution—would be unenforceable because it did not satisfy the UCC requirements.

Summary

I advise that a written contract for the purchase of any art or collectible item should include the following:

- the name, address, and telephone number of the dealer
- the date of the transaction
- a full description of the item being sold
- the price, including applicable taxes
- the payment terms, if any
- shipment terms, if the item is being shipped
- any express warranties by the dealer (see Chapter 2)
- any disclaimers of implied warranties (see Chapter 2)
- the dealer's repurchase policy, if there is one (see below)

2

Express and Implied Warranties Generally

Generally speaking, most legal problems arising from art and collectible transactions relate somehow to whether items conform to the seller's description, either in regard to their authenticity, type, quality, grade, rarity, or provenance. There are many traps here for the unwary buyer, and the key is to keep the risk of nonconformity on the dealer, so that in case of problems you can demand your money back or other compensation. The most important way to do this is by getting warranties, which are assurances from the dealer that the item is what it appears to be. Warranties are absolute, meaning that the dealer is responsible if the items do not conform, regardless of whether the dealer *knew* they did not conform at the time of sale or was in any way negligent in describing the items. Because the risk of "honest mistakes" falls on the dealer, breach of warranty is a very powerful legal tool for collectors and investors in art and collectibles.

As with the writing requirements, the UCC is the source of most of the relevant legal rules and principles applicable to warranties. Certain major art and collectibles market states have additional laws relating to warranties. The remainder of this chapter will discuss express warranties, implied warranties, dealer's ability to disclaim them, and the relevant statutes of limitations. Chapter 3 reviews specific warranties relating to art and collectibles.

Express Warranties versus Statements of Opinion

Express warranties are those made in writing or orally at or before the sale, and which become part of the contract. They are the warranties the seller makes directly to the buyer, as opposed to warranties which are implied by the nature of the transaction or by indirect statements by the seller. They are personal to the specific buyer and seller, and ordinarily they do not extend to subsequent owners of the goods. In other words, if you purchase art or collectibles with a warranty from the dealer, that dealer will not owe any warranty to someone else to whom you sell the goods later (even one day later). Under UCC §2-313, express warranties come in three categories: (1) affirmations of fact or promises relating to the goods; (2) descriptions of the goods; (3) a sample or model. If any of the above become "part of the basis of the bargain" between buyer and seller, the seller is expressly warranting that the goods will conform.

Whether or not particular statements by a seller are warranties is sometimes tricky, and over the years certain interpretations have been imposed upon the UCC's language. For example, sellers are permitted to engage in "puffing," *i.e.*, saying that the work they're selling is "the best" example of a particular artist or genre. Such a statement is considered a statement of opinion and not a warranty, meaning that the dealer will not have to back it up. Section 2-313 of the UCC defines statements of opinion as "an affirmation merely of the value of the goods or a statement purporting to be merely the seller's opinion or commendation of the goods."

In cases involving everything from used cars to bull calves, the courts have analyzed salesmen's pitches to determine whether or not particular statements became part of the purchase contract or were merely non-binding opinions. Judges seem to look at whether statements are the type on which purchasers in particular markets reasonably rely in making purchases. Most of us would agree that were we to buy a painting from a dealer who says it is "the best example I've ever seen from Picasso's 'blue period'" we would reasonably rely upon the fact that the painting is by Picasso, and perhaps that it dates from Picasso's "blue period," but not that it is "the best" from that period. On the other hand, in the rare coin market, a dealer's statement in writing that a particular coin is the "finest known" example of a particular date or variety would probably be binding on the dealer, because that term is reasonably relied upon by rare coin buyers. Generally speaking, statements relating to the quality, rarity, or provenance of art or collectible items are far more likely to be considered warranties and not opinions if they are unequivocal, in writing, and made prior to the purchase.

In some states, such as New York and California, special state laws help buyers of certain types of art and collectibles by abolishing the distinction between opinion and warranty in purchases from dealers. In addition to the UCC provisions above, New York Arts and Cultural Affairs Law §13.01 provides that when dealers in fine art multiples (including prints, photographs, and sculpture made in more than one copy) provide written "certificates of authenticity" or similar paperwork to their non-dealer customers, they expressly warrant all material facts contained in those documents. California Civil Code §1744.7 does likewise. This means that factual statements contained in written documentation from a dealer covered by those statutes is much more likely to be a warranty than an opinion. The statutes provide some small protection for dealers who act in good faith, however (see "Authenticity" section of Chapter 3). With respect to the warranty-opinion issues, however, New York's §13.01 specifically states that the "degree of warranty" given by a dealer in a certificate of authenticity is subject to the terminology used and the meaning accorded that terminology by the customs and usages of the trade at the time. I doubt that even under the New York statute a written statement that the Picasso was "the best I've ever seen" would be binding on a dealer. The primary differences between the New York and California statutes is, as we will see below, that California's applies to more inexpensive works than does New York's. Both states, however, reacting to chronic abuses in the sale of autographed sports collectibles, adopted legislation barring the "opinion" defense in such sales. New York Arts and Cultural Affairs Law §60.02 requires a written certificate of authenticity including identifying information about the dealer as well as an express warranty relating to the autograph, and states that these express warranties

> shall not be negated or limited . . . because any statement relevant to the autographed collectible is, or purports to be, or is capable of being, merely the dealer's or the supplier's opinion.

But don't forget that despite the legislation I've just described, a vast array of collectible items are subject to no mandatory express warranty requirements at all. Therefore, it is up to the buyer to insist that the dealer "put it in writing," and in such a way that the dealer must stand behind the key attributes of the item he or she is selling.

Implied Warranties

The UCC recognizes that what a seller *doesn't* say is sometimes more important than what he or she says in inducing the buyer to make a purchase. Dealers convey certain understandings to buyers about their goods in subtle ways, and it would be unfair in some instances to hold dealers only to what they actually tell customers. Consequently, certain "implied" warranties are part of the sale of goods even when they aren't expressed in any oral or written agreement. Because these warranties create obligations for the dealer without express language, and collectors and investors might not even be aware they exist, you should read this section carefully to fully understand your rights.

The most important implied warranty is the warranty of merchantability. UCC §2-314(2) states that "merchantability" includes "pass[ing] without objection in the trade under the contract description," being "fit for the ordinary purposes for which such goods are used," and "conform[ing] to the promises or affirmations of fact made on the container or label if any." As we have seen, New York and California have taken all ambiguity out of the sale of certain art and collectible items, but in most cases the dealer need not make any express warranties at all.

Recently, I attended a collectibles convention and saw a Matisse print being offered for sale. But the dealer did not actually *say* it was a Matisse. It was in Matisse's style and bore Matisse's signature, but the print was marked only with a price and no other description. I also saw many baseball cards which certainly looked to be authentic and in mint condition, but the dealer did not actually *say* that they were. Without some kind of warranty, a buyer might be unprotected against the risk that the print was fake or that the card was altered. This is where the implied warranty of merchantability comes in, giving buyers of art or collectible items legal rights if those items are determined to be fake, counterfeit, or otherwise not in accord with their description or appearance. In other words, even when a dealer has made no express warranties regarding authenticity, attribution, or quality, those types of warranties might be implied into the sale by virtue of the catch-all category of "merchantability."

Moreover, UCC §2-314(3) provides that additional implied warranties may arise from "course of dealing or usage of trade." That means that the usual practices of art and collectibles dealers in a particular area may be incorporated to some degree into all sales. Usages and practices are crucial to dealer-to-dealer trades, where only partial descriptions of items are sufficient for everyone to understand what is being sold. But they also play a role in retail transactions, because certain terms with specialized meanings in an art or collectibles area will bind the dealer not only to the specific words, but also to those words *as they are understood in the trade.*

A simple example from the rare coin field is the use of the term "uncirculated." For numismatists, the designation "uncirculated" means that a coin has had less than a certain level of wear or scratches. Although different grading standards are employed within the general classification "uncirculated," dealers and experts generally agree on the difference between uncirculated coins and circulated coins. A coin sold by a dealer as "uncirculated" must conform not just with the dealer's *subjective* interpretation of that term, but with the *objective* understanding of the term in the coin business. In other words, a coin which was purchased directly from the Mint but then handled carelessly by its owner might be "uncirculated" in a technical sense, but it would not pass the industry standards for an uncirculated grade.

Another implied warranty is that of "fitness for particular purpose," which derives from UCC §2-315. This applies when the seller knows that the goods are being bought for a particular purpose. Its application to art and collectibles is tenuous, at best. However, conceivably it could apply when a dealer sells a non-weatherproofed sculpture to someone planning to display it outdoors.

Disclaiming Warranties

All warranties created by the UCC can be disclaimed by dealers, but the disclaimers must conform to UCC requirements. UCC §2-316 provides guidelines for effectively disclaiming implied warranties.

The first guideline is that where possible, disclaimers will be interpreted so that they are consistent with language in other relevant documents from the dealer that create warranties. This means that a disclaimer may not work if other portions of the dealer's marketing materials appear to create the very warranties the dealer is trying to disclaim. For example, if a dealer gives express warranties of authenticity on the front of the invoice, he cannot disclaim those same warranties on the back of the invoice.

The second guideline for disclaimers is that the warranty of merchantability is disclaimed only by (1) referring to it specifically in a conspicuous written disclaimer; or (2) using terms such as "as is" which "calls the buyer's attention to the exclusion of warranties and makes plain that there is no implied warranty." The UCC specifically states that terms such as "seller disclaims all warranties, express and implied" will NOT disclaim the warranty of merchantability.

Many entirely reputable dealers place legalistic disclaimers in capital letters on their invoices. In the sale of certified rare coins, I have suggested that clients use disclaimers such as the following:

> Dealer sells coins certified by PCGS or NGC. Each of these coin grading services is recognized within the coin industry for its superior expertise, and each guarantees unequivocally that coins certified by it are authentic and unaltered. Dealer relies upon those guarantees in selling coins, and does not independently verify whether certified coins are authentic or unaltered. Accordingly, Dealer expressly disclaims any express or implied warranties otherwise attaching to the coins, including that the coins are merchantable.

As we will see in Chapter 9, auction houses have taken the disclaimer of warranties to their limits, and buyers who desire the protection of such warranties must still buy through retail dealers.

New York and California's mandatory warranties for retail sale of prints, sculptures, and autographed sports memorabilia are subject to special restrictions on disclaimers. New York will not enforce disclaimers in sales of fine art unless they are conspicuous and "in words which would clearly and specifically apprise the buyer that the seller assumes no risk, liability, or responsibility for the authenticity of the authorship of such work of fine art." The statute specifically negates attempted disclaimers where the work is later proven to be a counterfeit. For fine art and autographed sports collectibles, New York law states that express warranties cannot be "negated or limited" simply because a dealer did not intend that warranties be made.

Another way dealers can escape implied warranties is to give the buyer a chance to inspect the goods before entering into the contract. If the buyer either inspects or refuses the chance to do so, defects which the buyer ought to have found by his inspection are waived. However, this exception has only a limited application to normal retail purchases of art and collectibles for two reasons: (1) a return privilege after purchase will not be deemed the equivalent of a *pre-purchase* inspection; (2) the UCC states that "a nonprofessional buyer will be held to have assumed the risk only for such defects as a layman might be expected to observe." This means that if the defect with a particular item was obvious to an average, *non-expert* observer, a buyer who inspects the item prior to purchase accepts it with the defect and can't raise the defect later as grounds for rescinding the deal. Examples of defects which can be waived this way are hinges on unused stamps, heavy scratches on rare coins, tears in baseball cards and ink smears on lithographs. However, as we will see, most warranty claims relating to art and collectibles do not arise out of such "obvious" defects. Warranties of authenticity, designation, or authorship usually survive despite pre-purchase inspections.

Statutes of Limitation on Breach of Warranty Claims

Warranties don't last forever, and they shouldn't. In most cases the facts warranted by dealers about a product are either true or false as of the date of sale, and diligent buyers discover any discrepancies within a reasonable period of time. In addition, the UCC's express and implied warranty provisions force dealers to maintain back-up documentation for their warranties—or remember what they did or did not say to particular customers—

until they are absolutely sure they will not be sued, which is a burden. The absolute nature of UCC warranties—requiring full refunds regardless of whether the dealer was deceitful or even negligent—increases that burden. At some point, there needs to be closure. Accordingly, there is UCC §2-725, which gives buyers four years from the date of sale to bring suit for breach of any express or implied warranty.

This is a very important limitation on a buyer's rights under the UCC. Four years from the date of sale, a buyer loses his or her right to sue for breach of warranty. It does not matter when the buyer learns that there was a breach, and it often happens that defects are not discovered until the four-year period has already expired. The UCC provides no relief in these situations. So in *Firestone & Parson v. Union League of Philadelphia*, 833 F.2d 304 (3d Cir. 1987), an art dealer who had purchased a painting he had believed to be by Albert Bierstadt was barred from suing the seller five years after the sale when it became widely held that the painting was by a far less renowned artist and was only worth ⅒ of what the owner had paid. However, it is sometimes the case that dealers will accept returns of unauthentic items regardless of how much time has passed. Indeed, Malletts, an antiques dealer in London, recently discovered that a Russian gold dinner service it had sold a customer in 1978 was a fake, and refunded the customer's £1.5 million purchase price plus interest, fully aware that the buyer could no longer sue for a refund.

The only exception to the four-year UCC statute of limitations is for warranties which extend to future performance, in which case the limitations period does not start running until the future event does (or does not) take place. This exception rarely applies to the sale of art or collectibles, but it is occasionally offered. For example, I once represented a dealer in a breach of warranty case entitled *Hagen v. J.I. Corporation*, Civ. 88-1328L (W.D.N.Y. filed 9/21/88) in which the plaintiff claimed that certain rare coins were not of the "grade or quality" warranted by my client when she bought them. Plaintiff argued that because the coins were supposed to go up in value and didn't, she could sue seven years after the purchase. The court stated that if there were any warranties concerning grade or quality, they would have been breached at the time of sale, and "there was no 'performance' for plaintiffs to 'await.'" The claim was dismissed. In the art world, a typical case is *Rosen v. Spanierman*, in which plaintiffs purchased a painting represented to be by John Singer Sargent in 1968, received periodic appraisals from the dealer, and in 1987 learned from Christie's that the painting was a fake. The court refused to apply the "future performance" exception, essentially blaming the plaintiffs for having waited 19 years to have the painting appraised by someone other than the original dealer which, the court indicated, "is not an onerous burden." However, in a 1990 case, *Balog v. Center Art Gallery— Hawaii, Inc.*, a Hawaii federal judge indicated that art and collectibles were precisely the types of items for which a warranty of authenticity involved future performance, criticizing decisions such as the one in my coin case and *Rosen*:

> In the view of this court, far from being based on sound reasoning, these decisions flow from a too-literalistic application of the Code which takes no cognizance of the unique problem presented by the application of the UCC to artwork and other collectibles. . . . [I]n the case of artwork which is certified authentic by an expert in the field or a merchant dealing in goods of that type, such a certificate of authenticity constitutes an explicit warranty of future performance sufficient to toll the UCC's statute of limitations.

If this rule were applied to art and collectibles cases, the warranty of authenticity would, in effect, last for as long as the buyer holds the goods. I think the Hawaii decision is an aberration, however. The "future performance" exception is intended to deal with warranties which, by their very nature, might not be satisfied within four years, for example, tires warranted to last for 40,000 miles. A car owner who drives infrequently will not travel 40,000 miles in four years, but the future performance exception ensures that the dealer will still be responsible legally if the tires fail before 40,000 miles.

The state laws of New York and California discussed above do not, for the most part, extend the limitations periods that would otherwise apply. The important thing to remember is that the UCC relieves buyers of art and collectibles of the need to thoroughly research their purchases ahead of time, by imposing upon the dealer the responsibility for any mistakes. However, once the sale is consummated, the buyer must take care to verify any material facts about the item before four years have elapsed, or risk losing his or her right to get legal satisfaction from the dealer.

3

Warranties of Authenticity, Condition, and Rarity

Now that you've seen how express and implied warranties work generally, I will describe the specific warranties you should look for when buying art or collectibles, how they should be expressed, and their limitations.

Warranty of Authenticity/Attribution

The key warranty on art and collectible items is that of authenticity, sometimes called the warranty of attribution. By simply describing a painting as "Howard Behrens—Venetian Brilliance 1992," an art dealer makes several express warranties about the work: that it was painted by Howard Behrens; that it is the work entitled "Venetian Brilliance"; and that it was made (or at least published by Behrens) in the year 1992. And selling a rare record as an "original" of Elvis' "Good Rockin' Tonight" tells buyers that the record was manufactured by the company that first recorded the hit song (Sun Records), and that it is not a bootleg or subsequent re-recording. Through express and implied warranties, dealers always assure collectors and investors about the authenticity of what they are getting, and authenticity probably is the only warranty applicable to *all* art and collectible transactions.

As we have seen, terms contained in warranties are entitled to their literal meaning as well as to whatever special meaning is attributed to them in a particular area of the art and collectibles business. The art trade, for example, has certain distinctions relating to attribution which have been adopted as law in New York:

> Language used in a certificate of authenticity or similar written instrument, stating that:
> (a) The work is by a named author or has a named authorship, without any limiting words, means unequivocally, that the work is by such named author or has such named authorship;
> (b) The work is "attributed to a named author" means a work of the period of the author, attributed to him, but not with certainty by him;
> (c) The work is of the "school of a named author" means a work of the period of the author, by a pupil or close follower of the author, but not by the author.

Such phrases as "original," "mint state uncirculated," and "actual" may constitute express warranties of authenticity with respect to different types of collectibles. Moreover, because authenticity is the primary element of "merchantability," it is implied regardless of what the dealer may say. Often, simply associating an artist or celebrity with a particular item is enough to imply a warranty that the artist created the work or the celebrity owned or used the item. But don't rely on *implied* warranties of authenticity. If at all possible, warranties of authenticity should be express, and in writing.

Most art and collectibles dealers are honest and scrupulous in describing the goods they sell, but sometimes you'll need to insist on a full written description. For original art this means that the artist's name, the name of the work, the medium, and the date it was produced may appear on the invoice or on a document incorporated into the invoice. For rare coins, an authenticity description could include country name, denomination, date, mintmark, and variety. For stamps, Scott catalog number, color, watermark, perforation, and cancellation may be part of a warranty of authenticity. Many collectible items require more elaborate descriptions, because their value depends upon particular attributes or associations. Those attributes or associations must be clearly stated as part of a warranty of authenticity. For example, Bob Dylan's 1963 album *The Freewheelin' Bob Dylan* is relatively easy to obtain at classic record stores. So when Good Rockin' Tonight, a rare record auction house in Newport Beach, California, described a particular copy of the album with a minimum bid of $5,000, its description of the item included an explanation:

> After Bob Dylan refused to appear on the Ed Sullivan Show because CBS censors would not allow him to perform "Talkin' John Birch Society," either he or CBS (there are conflicting stories) had several cuts, including "Talkin' John Birch Society," deleted from his upcoming album. A few copies managed to escape with the 'censored' songs. It is estimated that fewer than ten copies of the mono version of this album exist. It is perennially at the top of the list of the world's rarest record album [*sic*].

In reviewing written warranties concerning authenticity and attribution, make sure they match whatever oral statements were made by the seller, and that they are unequivocal. Sometimes there is legitimate doubt about art or collectible items, as we will see below. But if the dealer tells you unequivocally that the boxing trunks you are buying were Rocky Graziano's, the invoice should not say they are "possibly" Graziano's. This is common sense—if a dealer will not put his oral statements concerning authenticity in writing, you should think twice about the purchase. Collectors and investors are presumed to have less knowledge than the dealer regarding facts and technical distinctions relating to authenticity, and you are, therefore, entitled to rely upon the dealer's warranties of attribution and authenticity and can hold the dealer liable if an item turns out to be a fake. The corollary of that rule, of course, is that if you are an expert in a particular area, you may not be able to rely upon a dealer's warranty of authenticity. In certain fields such as U.S. Colonial period coins, seasoned collectors are often better able to recognize counterfeits than some professional dealers. For such expert buyers, statements by the seller might not be "part of the basis of the bargain" and would not entitle the buyer to rescind the purchase.

As noted above, New York and California have led the nation in protecting purchasers of certain art and collectibles in their states. Specifically, New York requires dealers to give purchasers certificates of authenticity whenever they sell "visual art multiples," which is defined by New York Arts and Cultural Affairs Law §11.01.20 as follows:

> [P]rints, photographs, positive or negative, sculpture and similar art objects produced in more than one copy and sold, offered for sale or consigned in, into or from this state for an amount in excess of one hundred dollars exclusive of any frame or in the case of sculpture, an amount in excess of fifteen hundred dollars. Pages or sheets taken from books and magazines and offered for sale or sold as visual art objects shall be included, but books and magazines are excluded.

California Civil Code §§1742 *et seq.* is similar, but applies to all fine art multiples regardless of price. Both states require the dealer to make several disclosures in their certificates of authenticity, including (1) the artist's name; (2) if the name appears on the item, how it got there (*i.e.,* did the artist sign it, or at least authorize it to be put there?); (3) process used to manufacture it (*i.e.,* lithography, serigraphy, photographic process); (4) whether the artist was dead when the multiple was made; (5) certain specific information in the case of "limited editions," which will be discussed below; (6) the date the multiple was made.

New York and California require certificates of authenticity to be given to customers at the customer's request, or in any event before the sale is consummated. This means that a prospective buyer can ask for a certificate of authenticity without committing in any way to the purchase, just to see what the dealer is going to be warranting. Once the price is agreed and the sale consummated, a certificate of authenticity must be given regardless of whether the buyer asked for one. Moreover, these states require dealers to post signs in their places of business which contain the following information:

California:
California law provides for the disclosure in writing of certain information concerning prints, photographs, and sculpture casts. This information is available to you, and you may request to receive it prior to purchase.

New York:
Article fifteen of the New York arts and cultural affairs law provides for the disclosure in writing of certain information concerning prints, photographs, and sculpture. This information is available to you in accordance with that law.

Special protections are given buyers of multiples through the mails, presumably because it is not possible to inspect mail order items prior to purchase. Catalogues, advertisements, or other written material from dealers soliciting a direct sale of specific multiples must also include lengthy descriptions of the certificate of authenticity requirements for each state, and they must give buyers the right to return items within 30 days for a full refund if they are unhappy with anything contained in the certificate of authenticity.

California and New York also require certificates of authenticity for autographed sports memorabilia being offered at $25 or more, which must include the dealer's name, address, and signature as well as (1) a description of the collectible and the name of the sports personality who signed it; (2) the purchase price and date of sale, unless that information appears in a separate invoice; (3) an express warranty that the item is authentic; (4) whether the item is one of a limited edition, and if so, provide certain additional information (see below). The California statute, §1739.7(b), requires certain additional items not required in New York, including: (1) whether the dealer is surety bonded or otherwise insured against errors and omissions and if so, proof of bonding or insurance; (2) the last four digits of the dealer's resale certificate number (for California sales tax purposes); (3) whether the item was signed in the dealer's presence; and (4) whether the item was obtained or purchased from someone else and if so, the name and address of that person.

Beyond New York and California, no other states require certificates of authenticity for art or collectible items. If certificates are given voluntarily, of course, the statements in them may be express warranties under most states' laws. New York and California provide specific rules regarding such voluntary certificates of authenticity in the sale of fine art, imposing upon dealers who choose to make such statements the burden of having them construed as express warranties, rather than statements of opinion.

Attribution and authenticity issues sometimes become quite complicated, as dealers and consumers struggle in court over alleged breaches of warranties. Where one expert says that a work is genuine, and another disagrees, what are buyers and courts to do? The case of *Dawson v. G. Malina,* 463 F.Supp. 461 (S.D.N.Y. 1979) illustrates the point. Dawson purchased certain Chinese art objects from Malina, an art dealer, and for each object Malina stated from which imperial dynastic period it dated. For example, a large ceramic vase was attributed to the Sung Dynasty (960–1279), and two jade sculptures were attributed to the period of Chien Lung's rule as emperor (1736–1795). Dawson later showed the works to various experts who doubted that these attributions were correct, but Malina obtained opinions supporting his position and refused to accept return of the items. As the judge described it, Dawson and Malina each contended that the other had the burden of proving him dead wrong:

Dawson argues that unless it can be found that these works of art were unqualifiedly what defendants represented each of them to be, he is entitled to relief for breach of warranty. . . . [D]efendants maintain that unless Dawson has conclusively established by a preponderance of the evidence, that the representations made by them were in fact inaccurate, his claim for breach of warranty with respect to these pieces must fail.

The court adopted a standard more favorable to Malina (the dealer) than to Dawson. Noting that attributing works to a particular period of Chinese antiquity is an "inexact science" and "to a substantial extent a subjective judgment," the court determined that if there was a "reasonable basis in fact" for a representation at the time it is made, there is no breach of warranty.

What happens when a work which is universally believed to be authentic at the time of sale is later determined to be counterfeit or misattributed? This happens periodically with rare coins, and more and more often with fine art. A recent example occurred with a Mary Cassatt painting which was purchased from Sotheby's in 1987, but which the Cassatt authentication committee (which didn't exist until 1990) refused to authenticate in 1994. Sotheby's refused to refund the purchase price, and after litigation, a confidential settlement was reached. If a warranty of authenticity is absolute, a seller should always have to take back unauthentic items, at least until the statute of limitations expires. The question is whether the warranty is breached just because scholarly interpretations of authenticity change with time. New York Arts and Cultural Affairs Law §13.05 seems to say maybe, at least in some cases. For fine art multiples produced after 1900, and photographs produced after 1950, "the existence of a reasonable basis in fact for information warranted shall not be a defense to an action to enforce such warranty." So buyers of such works are protected. However, for pre-1900 prints or sculpture casts, or pre-1950 photographs, or any other forms of fine art or collectible item, a dealer with a reasonable basis in fact for stating that the work was authentic and properly attributed will prevail despite a change in scholarly opinion. California Civil

Code §1744.7 provides the same rule as New York's but is written in more direct terms:

> [W]ith respect to photographs and sculptures produced prior to 1950, and other multiples produced prior to 1900, as to information required by paragraphs (3), (4), (5), and (6) of subdivision (a) of Section 1744, the art dealer shall be deemed to have satisfied this section if a reasonable basis in fact existed for the information provided.

Where both parties act in good faith, the issue of changing interpretations is very difficult, and we will see in Chapter 9 that auction houses deal with it head on in their Terms and Conditions of Sale.

The importance of general opinion regarding authenticity has resulted in experts who deny the authenticity of works can find themselves being sued by owners of those works who fear that their opinions decrease or destroy the market value of those works. Probably the most famous art-related litigation in history, *Hahn v. Duveen,* related to whether a painting entitled *La Belle Ferronnière* was painted by Leonardo da Vinci. Harry and Andrée Hahn had brought the painting to the United States in 1920, and had announced its sale to the Kansas City Art Gallery for $250,000. A New York newspaper sent a reporter to get a quote from Sir Joseph Nuveen, a world-famous art dealer, who looked at a photograph of the painting and replied that the Hahns owned a copy, of which the original hung in the Louvre. The buyer cancelled the sale, and the Hahns sued Duveen, alleging that his comment made the painting worthless. Despite Duveen's free speech arguments, and a parade of experts supporting both sides, the trial ended in a hung jury and a settlement payment by Duveen. In a more recent case, an association of Jackson Pollock experts was sued by a dealer who contended that its refusal to certify a painting he wished to sell as a genuine Pollock caused Sotheby's and Christie's to refuse to handle the work. The case was dismissed on technical grounds, but the case illustrates the importance of experts in specific areas of the market.

Even where particular items are authentic in some respects, they may not be exactly as described. Probably the most peculiar example in the fine art area involved "Salvador Dali" lithographs. Apparently in his later years, Dali signed huge numbers of blank sheets. A gallery obtained thousands of these sheets, and persuaded relatives of Dali to "authorize" original Dali lithographs to be printed on them. The gallery then sold the lithographs to the public as genuine Dalis, relying upon the unquestionable fact that both the lithographs and the signatures were genuine.

However, the greatest abuses have been in the area of sports collectibles. For example, sports figures occasionally use members of their staffs, and even autographing machines, to sign their names to multiples of sports cards and other memorabilia, resulting in autographs which are *authorized,* but not *authentic.* New York has attempted to fight the potential for deception in this area through recent amendments to the Arts and Cultural Affairs Law which prohibit dealers from selling autographed merchandise if they know or have reason to believe that it was signed "other than by the sports personality in his or her own hand," and by laws which require dealers in autographed sports merchandise to expressly warrant authenticity, and to post the following disclosure in a conspicuous place near the merchandise:

SALE OF AUTOGRAPHED SPORTS MEMORABILIA AS REQUIRED BY LAW A DEALER WHO SELLS TO A CONSUMER ANY SPORTS MEMORABILIA DESCRIBED AS BEING PERSONALLY AUTOGRAPHED FOR TWENTY-FIVE DOLLARS OR MORE MUST PROVIDE A WRITTEN CERTIFICATE OF AUTHENTICITY AT THE TIME OF SALE.

California further protects buyers of autographed sports items by requiring dealers to disclose the following: (1) whether the item was autographed in the dealer's presence; (2) whether the item was obtained from a third party, and if so, the third party's name and address; and (3) whether the dealer is surety bonded or insured against errors and omissions, with proof. Note that these are disclosure requirements only. For example, dealers are not *required* to be bonded, but they are required to *disclose* whether or not they are.

Other authenticity problems result from the fact that authentic items sometimes demand premiums based on their association with particular individuals or events. For example, certain autographed sports memorabilia are far more valuable if they were "game used," *i.e.*, used by the athlete during his playing days. It occasionally happens that a particular item carries an authentic autograph, but was not "game used" as described by the dealer. A sports-card dealer once told me a story about a man who came to him with several baseball bats autographed by Roberto Clemente, the legendary Pittsburgh Pirates outfielder. He represented that the bats were "game used," but the dealer told him that he had doubts because the bats looked too pristine. The man took the bats away, but returned with them the next day. This time, the bats were scuffed from having hit a few baseballs. Similar problems attach to "treasure coins" and other artifacts associated with famous shipwrecks, as well as rock and roll memorabilia such as the guitars supposedly played by George Harrison or Jimi Hendrix, which sell for large sums at auctions and guitar shows. There may be no way to establish authenticity conclusively in such cases. The coins might legitimately have been from the time of the shipwreck but not been aboard, and Harrison or Hendrix might have owned guitars (or worked for recording companies which did), but not played them. In such cases, the buyer's only protection is the dealer's express warranty.

One last point about authenticity and collectibles. Counterfeiting of items such as coins and stamps is prohibited by federal law, and it is actually a crime to sell counterfeits of such items. In addition, associations of collectibles dealers have ethical guidelines which essentially require members to guarantee authenticity. For example, a rare coin dealer who is a member of the Professional Numismatists Guild (PNG) is prohibited from knowingly selling a counterfeit coin, and PNG members will always accept returns of such items. In addition, in Chapter 10 we will discuss remedies under the federal Lanham Act and the Hobby Protection Act for sale of counterfeit or "gray market" art or collectible items.

Warranties of Condition, Quality, Grade

The true value of authentic collectible items can often vary enormously depending upon their condition. An uncirculated coin, fully-centered stamp, or mint sports card is usually worth far more than a circulated, off-center, or wrinkled example of such an item. Even rare record albums are differentiated according to a detailed set of grading standards. Far more than authenticity, however, condition is subjective. Experts can all agree that a coin is authentic, and then all disagree as to its condition. In addition, each type of item has its own commonly used standards, interpretations, and terminology relating to condition. Buyers must understand what standards are applied with respect to that particular item, and what interpretations of those standards are used by dealers of such items, because those standards and interpretations will limit your rights against the dealer.

Here is an example. If a dealer sells you a coin described as an 1893-S Morgan Silver Dollar in Extremely Fine condition, at least two express warranties are being made: (1) the coin is an authentic 1893-S Morgan Dollar; (2) the coin is in Extremely Fine condition. Undoubtedly, most experts can agree as to whether, in fact, the date, mintmark, and type of the coin is correct. But is the coin in Extremely Fine condition? More importantly, will a buyer ever *know* whether it is or is not? In coin grading, subjectivity prevails. Even with uncirculated coins, where the Sheldon Scale purports to place all coins on a scale of 0 (badly worn) to 70 (perfect), experts will differ, sometimes significantly, about how a particular coin grades. A dealer once submitted the same group of uncirculated coins to 20 top dealers for grading, and for practically every coin, the range of reported grades was 3 or more on the 60–70 scale applied to uncirculated coins. And some major dealers refuse even to apply the Sheldon Scale, preferring their own "adjectival" grades such as "extremely fine" and "brilliant uncirculated." These terms don't have direct numerical equivalents.

Grading/condition controversies between dealers and collectors are uncommon with original works of art, but with rare coins, stamps, sports cards, and sports memorabilia they can be very difficult to resolve. Differing grading standards are employed by different dealers, and even those standards have been known to change over time. This confusing situation has frequently allowed unscrupulous dealers to mislead or deceive their customers. For example, in 1989 the FTC brought suit against a Florida rare coin dealer who advertised coins as priced "below wholesale." Interested buyers were shown the *Coin Dealer Newsletter*, a weekly price guide to dealer-to-dealer transactions in most types of rare coins. For each coin listed in the *CDN*, there were reported prices in all uncirculated grades, and this dealer's prices were below the *CDN*'s. How did he do it? By selling coins graded in accordance with a more liberal— less stringent—standard than was employed by the *CDN*. That meant that the coins the dealer called "MS-65s" would have been graded MS-62 or MS-63 by most other dealers. That meant that the value of the coins would be found not on the MS-65 line of the *CDN*, but with the MS-63s or MS-62s. Far from getting a bargain, the customers were actually paying double the true wholesale price of the coins.

Fortunately, today most rare coins can be graded by reputable third-party grading services such as Professional Coin Grading Service (PCGS) of Newport Beach, California, and Numismatic Guaranty Corporation (NGC) of Parsippany, New Jersey, who assign a grade and encase coins in tamper-evident plastic cases. The dealer can then warrant that a particular coin has been graded PCGS EF-45—extremely fine—a statement the truth of which can be proved objectively. But where the coins have not been third-party graded, confusion continues to reign among experts, and a buyer has only a slim chance of prevailing in a breach of warranty action based solely on grade.

With respect to sports memorabilia, the other major area where subjective measures of condition prevail, California has attempted to codify a definition of "mint condition" in 1995 amendments to California Civil Code 1739.7, as follows:

> "Mint condition" means any collectible sold on the open market or in a private transaction that meets all of the following requirements:
>
> (A) The item has never been circulated, used, or worn.
> (B) The item exhibits little or no signs of aging or degradation caused by oxidation or exposure to sunlight as a result of its display.
> (C) The item is otherwise free from creases, blemishes or marks.

This definition certainly eliminates circulated, faded, and otherwise defective items from the definition of "mint." It does not, however, resolve many grading issues relating to sports cards and memorabilia. It is best to buy from dealers who expressly warrant condition, and whose grades are backed either by a third-party service such as Professional Sports Authenticators (PSA) of Newport Beach, California, or by errors and omissions insurance. As we have seen, California requires dealers of autographed sports collectibles to disclose whether they are surety bonded or otherwise insured against errors and omissions.

Warranty of Rarity/Surviving Mintage

Part of the appeal of art and collectibles is their rarity, and market value is often based upon actual or perceived rarity. But rarity is relative when it comes to art and collectible items. A McDonald's prepaid telephone card which is one of 10,000 issued is relatively "common," as is a print from a series of

10,000. But if "only" 10,000 of a particular U.S. coin or stamp were ever issued, it would be rare indeed. On the other hand, modern commemorative coins and stamps minted by foreign governments in such numbers are not considered rare among dealers. Even the same items may be perceived as common by some people and rare by others. Such is the nature of the art and collectibles marketplace.

I will not attempt to explain concepts of rarity for particular art or collectible items, which is a book in itself. It is certainly beyond the scope of this one. But warranties relating to the rarity of art and collectibles are very important, and buyers promised "rare" or "limited edition" items need to know what to look for and expect. Certain federal and state laws provide guidance. For example, the U.S. Customs Service classifies only sculptures of 12 or fewer copies as "fine art" for purposes of duty-free entry into the U.S. The Visual Artists' Rights Act applies only to lithographs in editions of 200 or fewer. And California has two code sections which define the term "limited edition" without using any particular numbers. California Civil Code §1739.7(a)(6) defines "limited edition" sports collectibles as any item meeting the following requirements:

(A) A company has produced a specific quantity of a collectible and placed it on the open market.
(B) The producer of the collectible has posted a notice, at its primary place of business, that it will provide any consumer, upon request, with a copy of a notice that states the exact number of a collectible produced in that series of limited editions.
(C) The producer makes available, upon request of a consumer, evidence that the electronic encoding, films, molds, or plates used to create the collectible have been destroyed after the specified number of collectibles have been produced.

California Civil Code §1740 defines limited edition fine art prints as:

[F]ine art multiples produced from a master, all of which are the same image and bear numbers or other markings to denote the limited production thereof to a stated maximum number of multiples, or are otherwise held out as limited to a maximum number of multiples.

The definitions of "limited edition" just given will not be legally binding on a dealer selling other types of art or collectible items. However, every dealer's use of the term must be reasonable for the particular item and, where scarcity determines price, the dealer should give you an express warranty of some kind. As noted above, California and New York require express warranties for fine art prints and sculptures, but the extent of the warranty depends upon the type of art and its age. For example, for limited edition works made after January 1, 1983, both states' laws require disclosure not only of how many signed or numbered impressions were made, but also how many prior editions, contemporary unsigned/unnumbered impressions, artist's proofs, and publisher's proofs were made, and a warranty "that no additional multiples of the same image, including proofs, have been produced in this or in any other limited edition." For works made between 1950 and 1982, neither state requires disclosures relating to prior editions, and California does not require an express warranty that no other multiples were made, and New York does not require disclosure of the number of "proofs" made. The disclosure requirements lessen with older works, such that for works prior to 1900, neither state requires that the dealer disclose, much less warrant, the number in the edition. And dealers may disclaim knowledge of certain information required by the statutes, but they must do so expressly and "categorically" in the place where disclosure would otherwise be required so that, in the words of California Civil Code §1742(d): "the purchaser shall be enabled to judge the degree of uniqueness or scarcity of each multiple contained in the edition so offered."

I don't recommend paying a premium to buy any item classified as a limited edition without a specific written warranty of some kind from the seller regarding total number in the edition.

Another rarity issue is survivability. With respect to contemporary lithographs or "commemorative" plates, the number of extant copies is easy to determine. Certain other collectibles, however, are rare not because they were *made* in small quantities, but because they *exist today* in small quantities. Such items as rare coins, stamps, and antiquities fall into this category. Mintage is often irrelevant in valuing such items, and the seller should give an express warranty as to *surviving* mintage. There are also "condition rarities," *i.e.*, items which are rare only by virtue of their fine state of preservation. Many of a particular Barbie doll may exist, but only a few in their original, unopened box. These are indeed "rare," but buyers who pay a premium for condition rarities are assuming the risk that the majority of other collectors in that genre will also recognize that such items are worth more. A major problem with condition rarities, or with any collectible whose value depends upon a low survival rate, is that often we cannot verify the survival figures, and new discoveries depress the market price tremendously. An Egyptian dodechadrachm was sold for $200,000 when it was believed to be unique. Once a "hoard" of 18 more was discovered, however, its value immediately dropped substantially. In investigating a Southern California rare coin investment firm on behalf of the Professional Numismatists Guild, I saw the following language in the firm's salesmen's scripts:

> [T]he population of this coin at this grade by PCGS is only __ meaning the amount of coins graded thus far at this grade by PCGS is only __. Meaning there are only __ in existence by PCGS at this grade and this is one of them.

This statement was deceptive. The script did not mention that PCGS was just one of three major grading services, that a large number of rare coins are held in private collections and are ungraded by any grading service, and that many less valuable coins aren't graded because for those coins third party grading isn't cost-effective. The clear intent of this script was to gloss over the truth in order to suggest to the investor that the dealer was expressly warranting rarity. The key to purchasing limited edition items is to have a firm written warranty from the seller as to just how rare the item is, and according to a standard of rarity recognized in the particular industry.

Summary

Remember that authenticity is the most common source of problems for buyers of art and collectibles, and keep the following principles in mind:

- demand that dealers give you specific, written warranties relating to authenticity
- understand the jargon used in different collecting areas before you buy
- when buying sports collectibles, ask to see the certificates of authenticity and other disclosures required by state consumer protection laws, and don't buy from dealers who don't comply
- be familiar with how condition affects value of particular items, and look for items which have been graded or appraised by independent, third-party organizations rather than just by the dealer
- when buying "limited edition" items, understand how that concept differs among different collecting areas, and before paying a premium for any rare item, be sure that the premium is justified by the *market's* definition of rarity
- if an item is thought to be authentic at the time of sale, you will probably bear the risk that later changes in scholarly opinion will reduce the value of that item

4

Getting Good Title

Nobody would buy a house without making sure the seller had legal title. Home buyers, through their attorneys or title insurance companies, do a title search, *i.e.*, a review of officially recorded documents to verify that the property is unencumbered and belongs to the person offering it for sale. With art and collectibles, unfortunately often there are no official title documents to review. And because stolen items or items of questioned title may be off the market for years, disputes over title may lie dormant until the item resurfaces. This chapter explains the more common issues relating to title to art and collectibles, and how to protect yourself as either a buyer or a seller.

Warranties of Title

UCC §2-312 provides that

> (1) . . . [T]here is in a contract of sale a warranty by the seller that (a) the title conveyed shall be good, and its transfer rightful; and (b) the goods shall be delivered free from any security interest or other lien or encumbrance of which the buyer at the time of contracting has no knowledge.

(2) A warranty under subsection (1) will be excluded or modified only by specific language or by circumstances which give the buyer reason to know that the person selling does not claim title in himself or that he is purporting to sell only such right or title as he or a third person may have.

The drafters of the UCC put it beautifully when they noted that this section "makes provision for a buyer's basic needs," namely "a good, clean title" given "in a rightful manner so that he will not be exposed to a lawsuit in order to protect it." In a nutshell, the UCC allows good faith buyers of art or collectibles to presume that the items they are buying either belong to the seller, or may be sold by the seller without claim by anyone else.

The warranty of title is implied into every sale, meaning that it is part of the contract even if it is not mentioned either orally or in writing. However, a warranty of title can be disclaimed, although that is quite rare in the sale of art or collectibles (we'll see an example in Chapter 9 on auctions).

The presumption of good title provided by UCC §2-312 is not an absolute guarantee that no third party will ever claim the goods. It is only a guarantee that if such a claim does arise, the buyer can claim against the seller for breach of the warranty. Ideally, when a third party shows that a sculpture you purchased three years ago is rightfully his, you would return the sculpture and recover your entire purchase price (plus interest) from the dealer. The reality of warranties of title is not nearly so good, however. A warranty is only as strong as the person giving it, and many dealers simply cannot easily refund a customer's purchase price. Also, as we will see, while UCC §2-725 limits claims for breach of the warranty of title to four years from the date of sale, title claims can arise long thereafter. So when buying antiquities or other items which often have dubious origins, it is best to get extensive provenance information and, better yet, to do business only with the most reputable dealers in the field.

Title to Stolen Items

It is an axiom of the law that nobody can pass good title to stolen goods. The true owner of an item may always recover it from its current holder, no matter how many times the item changed hands in between. Recently, I represented a rare coin dealer one of whose rarest U.S. $20 gold piece had been shipped by overnight courier to a New York dealer but never arrived there. Several months after that incident, my client was offered *his* coin at a coin show, and he traced it back through a chain of dealers to a dealer in New York who had bought it over the counter from someone who was obviously not a collector and for half its value. My client can recover the coin from whoever possesses it. While people who buy stolen art and collectibles in good faith (having no reason to think they were stolen) can almost always claim their money back from the dealer who sold them the items, they never acquire good title and they must surrender the goods to the true owner if a timely claim is made. So in my case the coin had to be surrendered, and the dealers along the chain of possession each claimed their purchase price from the one before them. Without such a rule, victims of theft could not be adequately protected, because thieves could put stolen items out of reach by selling them to innocent purchasers.

I deliberately used the words "timely claim" in the preceding paragraph. Most states have statutes of limitations governing claims for replevin, *i.e.*, recovery of stolen property, such as the three-year statute in New York. Oftentimes, stolen art and collectibles end up in private collections, out of public view for considerable periods of time, such as the Chagall gouache that disappeared from the Guggenheim Museum in New York in 1965 and reappeared in a private art collection in 1985. Moreover, for priceless works of art, a thief might well wait out the limitations period before selling his loot. This can result in injustices, and occasionally a statute of limitations is modified. For example, in many states a "discovery rule" suspends running of the limitations period until the victim locates the stolen item.

With a discovery rule, a three-year limitations period would not even begin until the true owner found the item and knew against whom to assert his or her claim. But fear of claims being brought decades after a theft led states to modify the modification, and require the true owner to prove that he or she exercised due diligence in looking for the item, barring which the claim would be denied. This is still the rule in certain states, including Indiana, the site of *Greek Orthodox Church v. Goldberg*, a landmark case involving stolen Byzantine mosaics, which I'll discuss in the context of "cultural property" later in this chapter.

In art market states, the courts feared that placing the burden of proof of due diligence on the original owner encourages thefts, by making it easier for thieves to "cleanse" their crime by keeping stolen art away from the market for several years. In New York, the law is that an innocent purchaser of stolen art or collectibles will prevail only if he can prove that the true owner knew where the items were and unreasonably delayed in bringing suit. In California, the true owner has three years to sue once he or she has discovered "the whereabouts" of the stolen work.

"Voidable" Title to Consigned Goods

The rules governing stolen property are logical and easy to understand. But what happens when the items aren't stolen, but someone claiming to be their owner says he or she was never paid in full for them? I was involved in a nationally publicized court case involving a Western painting. The owner of the painting had consigned it to a dealer on condition that if the dealer could not sell it within a certain period of time, the dealer had to buy it at an agreed price. The dealer tendered a check and, when the time period expired, the owner deposited the check. The check bounced. The owner telephoned the dealer and discovered that the painting had been resold (for a fair price) to an art collector who was unaware of the bounced check. The dealer had spent the money from the sale and was broke, so the owner sued the collector for return of the painting.

The collector got to keep the painting. This is a clear example of what lawyers call "voidable title." Think of it this way—

should the collector pay for the consequences of the dealer's bad check? In law, the bounced check will not impair the dealer's power to convey good title to the collector for two reasons.

First, the check bounced after the sale and after title had already passed. If the sale of a work of art could be rescinded because a seller has not yet paid the consignor, it would mean the end of the great public auction houses, who convey title to hundreds of millions of dollars of artwork each year, but may pay consignors as much as 30 to 45 days after they themselves are paid. Bidders at a Sotheby's or Christie's auction would be reluctant to risk their money if a subsequent payment dispute between the auction house and the consignor could result in their having to return the artwork. A bounced check from a dealer is a risk assumed by someone who wishes the benefits of consigning to a dealer, and, as we'll see later in Chapter 6, that risk can be mitigated by working with a financially secure dealer or making appropriate security arrangements. Even dealers selling works consigned by the original artists have the power to convey good title to good faith purchasers regardless of whether the dealers subsequently pay the artists, despite the fact that in many states dealers hold such works in trust for the artist by statute. In the case of the Western painting, the original owner assumed the risk that the dealer would transfer title before meeting all the payment terms of their consignment agreement.

Second, even if the dealer's check had bounced *before* the collector bought the painting, the collector was not aware of that fact and there was no reason for the collector to suspect that the dealer was not the authorized seller of the painting. There is a crucial distinction between "void" and "voidable" title. We have seen that had the painting been stolen from its owner the dealer would have had void title and could convey nothing to the collector or anyone else. However, the dealer did not steal the painting. The owner authorized him to have the painting and to sell it. Therefore, at a minimum the dealer had voidable title. The UCC specifically deals with this type of situation in UCC §2-403(1)(b), which states that a person who receives delivery of goods in a transaction of purchase may transfer good title to a good faith purchaser "even though . . . the delivery was in exchange for a check which is later dishonored." The collector acted in good faith and without knowledge that the sale to him was in violation of the rights of the owner or any third party. He bought the painting for a fair market price from a recognized art dealer. This is an everyday commercial transaction, the type the UCC intends to facilitate with its protection of good faith purchasers. As the New York Court of Appeals stated in the case of *Porter v. Wertz,* a case involving consignment of a Utrillo painting:

> The "entruster provision" of the Uniform Commercial Code is designed to enhance the reliability of commercial sales by merchants (who deal with the kind of goods sold on a regular basis) while shifting the risk of loss through fraudulent transfer to the owner of the goods, who can select the merchant to whom he entrusts his property.

It is important to note under what circumstances a buyer of art or collectibles is not an "innocent" or "good faith" purchaser entitled to the protection of the "entruster rule." In *Porter,* for example, the dealer purchased the Utrillo from someone he knew to be a delicatessen employee and not an art dealer who, it turned out, had obtained the painting by tricking the owner. And in *Taborsky v. Maroney,* the dealer purchased a Grant Wood drawing for $205,000 from another dealer knowing that the owners of the drawing had told him they wouldn't accept less than $400,000 for it.

Provenance Representations

Reputable dealers of art and collectibles know that buyers want good title, and whenever possible, they will research the provenance of unique or unusual items and provide the results of that research to the buyer at the time of sale. You'll recall from the previous chapter that for some items, the provenance is everything because the value is entirely in the item's association with a particular person or event. Provenance is also quite important in verifying title, because an item which was held in a major collection for decades, or traded openly among major dealers or auction houses, is unlikely to have been stolen. On the other hand, an item for which no provenance is available is questionable, especially where the dealer refuses to disclose how he or she obtained it.

Careful buyers demand express, written representations relating to provenance. Indeed, some experts contend that buyers of art and collectibles should inquire into provenance, and should be considered "good faith" buyers only if they do so diligently. This is not the law in any U.S. state. Indeed, in the *Porter* case I referred to earlier, the Art Dealers Association of America filed an *amicus curiae* brief "arguing that the ordinary custom in the art business is not to inquire as to title and that a duty of inquiry would cripple the art business. . . ." Of course, it makes good sense to inquire into title before making a major purchase. But if you buy from a reputable dealer, you may rely on the absence of unusual circumstances to protect your title to art or collectibles from claims by prior owners.

Buying Cultural Property

This is an increasingly difficult area of the art law field, and it is so intertwined with politics, religion, and national attitudes that whole books could be devoted to it. My focus will be on the problems which may be associated with purchasing certain types of art or antiquities which have been specially classified under international treaties or U.S. federal and state law.

Much of the world's most famous collections of ancient art and artifacts were acquired by theft during periods when European countries controlled areas of Greece, Egypt, and the Far East. Here's an example. Several months ago, an exhibition of Trojan gold jewelry and artifacts opened in Moscow. These treasures were excavated in Turkey by Heinrich Schliemann, the great German archaeologist credited with discovering the site of ancient Troy in modern day Turkey. Schliemann bequeathed the items to the German government, but in 1945, in the aftermath of World War II, Russian soldiers removed them from a Nazi hiding place and took them to Russia. The governments of Turkey, Germany, and Russia have declared that the items are their "cultural property." In this country, a huge amount of Native American material has been excavated and removed without knowledge or consent of the peoples involved. And so on throughout the world.

The growing power of Third World nations, combined with feelings of guilt among the major powers, has led to certain international and domestic legislation regulating the trade in what are called "cultural property." Anyone interested in buying antiquities or items of obvious historic, cultural, or religious significance should understand certain basic principles. First, what is cultural property? The term is defined in compromise fashion in some of the federal laws on the subject. The Customs Service's definition is codified in 19 CFR §12.104 to include (1) objects of "archeological interest" at least 250 years old; (2) objects of "ethnological interest" that originated with "tribal or non-industrial" societies and are "important to the cultural heritage of a people"; (3) a catch-all category which includes property "relating to history," pieces of historic monuments, antiquities and coins over 100 years old, postage stamps, furniture items over 100 years old, rare books and manuscripts, and original paintings, sculptures, engravings and prints.

Second, is it legal to own cultural property? Sometimes. Beyond that truism, however, there are some signs buyers should look for to avoid the risk of having their purchases taken from them. While it is legal to *own* certain items, it might not be legal to *import* them. In 1983, the U.S. enacted the Convention on Cultural Property Implementation Act, 19 U.S.C. §2601, which implemented into U.S. law the 1970 UNESCO Convention on the Means of Prohibiting and Preventing the Illicit Import, and Export, and Transfer of Ownership of Cultural Property. This law joined the U.S. in an international effort to restrict importation of items which other countries have declared to be illicitly obtained cultural property. Traditionally, the U.S. did not honor the laws of other countries in this area, and for that reason art dealers, collectors, and museums were able to acquire and import works which could not legally have been exported from their countries of origin. Ironically, the ardent opposition of art dealers to enactment of the UNESCO Convention into U.S. law was overcome only by the realization that many U.S. Customs officials were zealously stopping items of cultural property on the authority of the National Stolen Property Act, and that the Convention might restrict those officers to seizing only specified categories of goods.

The upshot of all this is that items of cultural property which were not legally exported from their country of origin cannot legally be imported into the U.S. Foreign countries maintain lists of such works, as well as of works which have been reported stolen from their museums or sacred sites. Items which make it into the U.S. are not affected by the law. They are, however, subject to state laws requiring replevin of stolen property, as we'll see below in the case of the Cypriot mosaics.

One of the burning controversies in the art world today relates to a new international convention prepared by UNIDROIT, another international organization. The UNIDROIT convention allows private actions against "possessors" of stolen or illegally exported cultural property, which would include museums, art restorers, and dealers or auction houses holding goods on consignment. Such items are confiscated without any compensation to their owners unless the owner can prove good faith. Art dealers are incensed that the Convention essentially requires signatory countries to enforce other countries' definitions of both "cultural property" and "illegal export," no matter how much those definitions might differ from those in the enforcing country. The Dutch government recently was told that if it ratified the UNIDROIT Convention, the huge Maastricht Art Fair would have to leave The Netherlands for a "safer" country where art items could not be seized. The U.S., Britain, and Germany have indicated that they will not sign, but only time will tell.

UNIDROIT notwithstanding, when it comes to Native

American art or artifacts, U.S. federal and state laws protect sites and require identification and return of any illicitly acquired property. I'll mention just a few of the major laws in this area: Pre-Columbian Monument Act, 19 U.S.C. §2091, Native American Graves Protection and Repatriation Act (NAGPRA), 25 U.S.C. §§3001 *et seq.*, and the New Mexico Cultural Properties Act, NMSA 18-6-1. Under NAGPRA, for example, Native American sacred objects and items of cultural patrimony excavated or discovered after November 1990 must be returned to the tribe upon whose land they were found, or another tribe with "close cultural affiliation" to the items. However, an organized tribal group must assert rights to particular items. If they do not, finders of the items may keep them. This law, and the fact that Native American tribes often don't have the capacity or the desire to maintain and preserve artifacts, has led some to challenge the entire concept of federal intervention in the art field. A 1989 article in *Archaeology* magazine estimated that thieves had ransacked at least 90 percent of the known archaeological sites in the Southwest, and that the number of looting incidents had increased 1,000 percent between 1980 and 1987. But *Art & Auction* reported (November 1994) about thousands of pottery vessels and human remains recovered during a freeway project in Arizona in 1991. The vessels and remains were delivered to the Tohono O'odhom tribe in accordance with federal law, but soon thereafter, they began appearing in galleries from Scottsdale to New York, and the Arizona State Museum was contacted by someone who had purchased some of the pottery from Native Americans going door to door. "It's the ultimate recycling," *Art & Auction* quoted Clement Meighan, a UCLA professor, as saying. "The government returns items to Indians, who turn around and sell them again. People who buy the artifacts are arrested, and the items wind up back with the Indians again. So much for sacred objects when up against the sacred dollar."

Even if works are not technically "cultural property" under the international treaties or federal statutes, because they were imported into the United States prior to enactment of the relevant laws, they may still be subject to common law replevin principles in the state where they are located. A good example of this is the landmark case of *Greek Orthodox Church of Cyprus v. Goldberg,* where an Indianapolis art dealer paid over $1 million to purchase Byzantine mosaics which turned out to have been looted from a church in Cyprus in the aftermath of the civil war there in the mid-1970s. The government of Cyprus relied upon Indiana law in bringing suit in 1989 to recover their stolen personal property. The court awarded the mosaics back to Cyprus, rejecting the dealer's arguments that the government did not use due diligence and that as an innocent purchaser, return of the mosaics would be unjust:

> Lest this result seem too harsh, we should note that those who wish to purchase art work on the international market, undoubtedly a ticklish business, are not without means to protect themselves. Especially when circumstances are as suspicious as those that faced Peg Goldberg, prospective purchasers would do best to do more than make a few last-minute phone calls. As testified to at trial, in a transaction like this, "All the red flags are up, all the red lights are on, all the sirens are blaring."

One final word on cultural property for those thinking of buying art abroad. Some foreign countries restrict export not only of important works which originated there, but any important work present within their boundaries. For example, until recently Argentina did not allow any works of art to leave at all. And in a celebrated case in 1995–96, the French government was required to pay dearly for its export restrictions. Apparently in 1989, France declared Van Gogh's *Jardin à Auvers* a "historical monument" which could not be exported. At the time, the painting was in France, having been brought there by its owner, Swiss national Jacques Walter. Walter eventually sold the painting at auction in Paris for $10.2 million, but sued the government, claiming that the sale price was severely reduced by the export restriction. The court awarded Walter $29 million which, according to published reports, is almost two years' budget for the Musées Nationaux in France.

5

Buying Art and Collectibles for Investment

It's human nature to hope that the things we collect will increase in value over time. However, in recent years art and collectibles have been bought by investors who are primarily interested in profits, or sold by dealers who tout their value as investments. Investors are often not as knowledgeable about art and collectibles as are collectors, and a profit motive sometimes obscures common sense and good judgment. This chapter alerts would-be investors to some common areas of trouble when buying art or collectibles for investment, and it explains some basic rights you may have as an investor. But remember an important distinction between this chapter and Chapters 2 and 3: All buyers of art and collectibles are entitled to enforce dealers' express and implied warranties, but those who buy for investment have certain *additional* rights.

Misrepresentations versus Literal Truth

It is unlawful to sell art and collectibles as investments by inducing investors to overpay for those items with misrepresentations of material fact. "Misrepresentations" are statements of fact which are untrue at the time they are made. As we saw with express warranties, art and collectible items invite statements of subjective opinions by dealers and subjective interpretations of those statements by the buyer. *Statements of opinion* which turn out to be untrue are not misrepresentations. Recall the example from Chapter 2 of the dealer who says that a painting is "the best" work from Picasso's "blue period." If the work was, in fact, from the blue period, the fact that another art expert—or *most* art experts—disagree that it is "the best" does not make the dealer's statement a misrepresentation. Likewise, as with express warranties of authenticity, if the statement was true at the time based on available knowledge and scholarship, the fact that it is subsequently proven false does not convert a good faith statement into a misrepresentation.

Notwithstanding the above, investors are often deceived by statements of fact which, though literally true, are misleading without additional information. The sales pitches of fraudulent retailers of art and collectibles are full of such half-truths and misleading statements. The law recognizes this, and consequently, the *omission* of necessary factual information is the equivalent of an outright misrepresentation where the dealer should have known that the result would be statements that are misleading to the average investor.

Here are some examples of truths, untruths, half-truths, and statements of opinion relating to the sale of rare coins:

- "This 1751 coin is from the sunken treasure ship *Vliegenhart.*" Because the *Vliegenhart* sank in 1735, this statement is untrue and is a misrepresentation.
- "This 1994 Lincoln Cent is the only one certified MS-65 by PCGS." Again, assuming this is literally true, it is nevertheless misleading in implying rarity, because the coin is extremely common. In fact, a 1994 penny is worth so little in any condition that the expense of independent PCGS certification is not justified (which, of course, means there aren't going to be many certified).
- "This 1894-S Barber Dime is the only one certified MS-65 by PCGS." Assuming the statement is literally

true, the implication that the coin is quite rare is not misleading because the 1894-S dime is one of the rarest U.S. coins.

The dealer's intent regarding the misrepresentation—*i.e.*, whether he *knowingly lied*—is relevant in certain ways, as we will see below, but does not affect whether an untrue factual statement is a misrepresentation. Nor, as we have seen, does it affect whether the dealer has breached the express or implied warranties we discussed in Chapters 2 and 3. However, for a misrepresentation to constitute investment fraud, as opposed to a breach of warranty, the dealer must have made the statement in bad faith. In the past, the doctrine of "negligent misrepresentation" might have made dealers liable for statements they honestly believed were true, because they "should have known" or with due diligence "could have known" the statements were false. Today, the rule generally followed by the courts is that a misrepresentation must be made either (1) with knowledge that it is false or (2) with a reasonable likelihood combined with "conscious avoidance" of the truth. This means, for example, that an art dealer who has good reason to think a particular work is a fake cannot rely entirely on the prior owner's representation that it is genuine, if authenticity could be easily checked.

Materiality and Reliance

Not every false statement of fact in connection with the sale of an item for investment is grounds for legal liability. Even if a misrepresentation is made intentionally, it must be "material," *i.e.*, it must relate to something a reasonable buyer would consider important to his or her decision to buy. In other words, if a dealer accurately describes and prices a painting to you, but lies about where he went to college, that would not be a material misrepresentation, unless the dealer's false statements about college included acquiring special expertise in the particular genre of work being offered.

In addition to materiality, the misrepresentation must actually have been reasonably relied upon by the investor prior to making the purchase. Investors who are disappointed with the performance of particular items cannot search the dealer's marketing materials with a fine-toothed comb looking for any possible falsehood upon which to demand their money back. The reliance requirement also means that statements made after the purchase are usually not actionable (a clear exception applies to statements made during a return period, upon which the investor relies in deciding to keep the goods).

Proof of materiality and reliance sometimes depends upon the knowledge and sophistication of the buyer. The more knowledgeable an investor is, the less "reasonable" is his or her reliance upon a dealer's representations. This sounds unfair, but the law only punishes dealers whose false statements of material fact *cause* the investor's damages. An investor who knows he or she is being lied to cannot use that fact as "insurance" against poor performance of the goods, keeping them if the market goes up and suing the dealer for misrepresentation if the market drops. I once represented a rare coin dealer against someone whose other investments included gold and cattle futures, resort condominiums throughout the world, and classic Mercedes-Benz sports cars. However, I also have represented investors who bought art and collectibles with little to no knowledge of investments. The law takes into account that less knowledgeable investors are more easily fooled.

Pricing (and Overpricing) Art and Collectibles for Investment

Beyond both materiality and reliance, an investor must also show that the misrepresentations resulted in his or her over-paying for the item. Most investment fraud claims relating to art or collectibles are brought after the investor learns that the item is not worth what he or she paid for it. But that could be caused by a drop in the item's market value since the time of purchase. The investor must prove that the difference is due to the item having been overpriced when he or she bought it.

This principle bears repeating. Even if the investor can prove that he or she relied upon the dealer's material misrepresentations about an item, if the dealer charged a fair price for the item there is no investment fraud. No harm, no foul. A breach of warranty claim would still exist, and the buyer might be entitled to return the item for his or her money back. But the claim would have to be made in accordance with the restrictions and statutes of limitations which apply to warranty claims. Without overpricing, an investment fraud claim simply does not exist.

While valuing particular art and collectibles is far beyond the scope of this book, it is common sense that the greater any item is marked up over its fair market value, the more the market value of the item must rise for the investor to sell at a profit. Investors must understand that there is a retail markup on every art or collectibles purchase. Dealers are not charities, and they are entitled to make a profit. In addition, in many cases, special premiums for art and collectible items are quite justified. Overpricing occurs in two instances: (1) when the markup is so high that the dealer's representations regarding level of investment risk and appreciation potential become misleading or false; (2) when the dealer's representations about pricing itself are false. In either case, the goods must be marketed as investments, not simply as collectible items. As Barry Cutler, former director of the FTC Bureau of Consumer Protection, used to say, a dealer can sell pencils for $1,000 apiece. However, Cutler quickly pointed out that if the pencils were sold as *investments*, the FTC would require that all material representations were correct.

The basics of art and collectibles pricing are simple. To the wholesale (dealer-to-dealer) price of the item, the dealer adds a markup reflecting his or her overhead and profit and, occasionally, the commission paid to a broker, financial planner, or consultant. "Wholesale value" can be loosely defined as the price one knowledgeable dealer would pay another for the item. This price consists of either an item's intrinsic value (in the case of gold and silver bullion items such as Kruger-rands, which sell at little to no premium), the "bid" price reported on market exchanges (such as the Certified Coin Exchange for numismatic coins) or in dealer trade publications, or a recent auction price indicative of market value. When an item is fairly illiquid (as are many art or collectible items), wholesale value is measured by what an investor who owned the item would get for it if he had a reasonable time to show it around in the marketplace. Remember that wholesale value is only one determinant of *fair market value.* Dealers are entitled to a fair markup over wholesale value, although what is "fair" depends upon a great many things, including services provided by the dealer, inventorying costs, market volatility, and credit terms. A dealer who searches out a particular painting or rare stamp for a customer may be entitled to more than one who takes one of a thousand Krugerrands in his vault and hands it over (although one shouldn't underestimate the costs of maintaining large inventories, even of common items).

But regardless of how much the dealer marks up an item for retail sale, investors in art and collectibles nearly always must sell at wholesale prices, unless they are prepared to consign their property and wait a considerable time to be paid. That means that in order to be promoted as low-risk investments, the markups must be such that the investor can profit in a moderate market upswing. As the court put it in *FTC v. Solomon Trading Co., Inc.,* 1994 Trade Regulation Reports ¶70,627, a case involving fraudulent sales of Erté lithographs: "[W]hen an investment has to double or triple in value before any gain can be realized, it is neither a good investment nor a low-risk investment." In that case, the court found that the dealer had marked up the lithographs 100 percent over their wholesale price, and charged clients 10 percent commission on resale, and that this made the dealer's representations regarding profit potential deceptive.

Generally speaking, art and collectibles are sold for 10 to 100 percent over their wholesale value. Bullion items carry the smallest markups, followed by rare coins and stamps, and proceeding to higher markup items such as art and antiquities. The costs of maintaining illiquid inventory, and the need to find the "right" buyer in order to maximize price, discourage dealers from paying high prices to stock even the works of art they themselves previously sold. Likewise, investors should be skeptical of dealers who say they are retailing art or collectibles at "below wholesale." In such cases, industry grading and pricing standards usually have not been met. FTC consumer pamphlets frequently quote the old adage: "If it sounds too good to be true, it probably isn't." Investors should also be skeptical of claims that daily shifts in the collectibles market require prompt action to "lock in" at a low price. Collectibles, other than items such as modern coins whose value is pegged to world gold and silver prices, rarely fluctuate much in value from day to day. And feverish claims by salespeople are intended also to suggest that selling will be easy when the time comes. It usually isn't.

This brings me to the subject of the premiums themselves. Investors need to understand the amount of premium, its justification, and whether the general marketplace also recognizes it. I received a Disney products catalogue recently. In it are numerous "limited edition" products, such as a "Pooh 30th Anniversary Coin," described in the catalogue as follows:

Edition
3,000
Limit

NEW POOH 30TH ANNIVERSARY COIN
Proof-quality, one troy-ounce .999 silver. This **Catalog Exclusive** numbered, limited edition medallion commemorating Winnie the Pooh and the Honey Tree is dated 1966–1996 and double-struck with Disney art from Pooh's first film. Pooh (as raincloud) balloons to the honey . . . enjoys a smackeral on reverse. 1½" diameter. Liberty Mint mark. **Edition: 3,000.** Velvet box. **Certificate of Authenticity. $75**

The intrinsic value of a one-ounce silver coin was approximately $5.00 on the day I received the catalogue. So the buyer of this coin is paying a $70 premium. For a collector who doesn't plan to sell, perhaps having the coin (and the velvet box) is worth it. But the catalogue description is addressed toward someone thinking about the coin as an investment. The number minted and the Certificate of Authenticity are only relevant to someone who is thinking ahead to selling the coin (after all, the catalogue comes from Disney itself, so the item is surely "authentic"!). Given the intrinsic value, the velvet box, the fact that only 3,000 were minted, *and* the Certificate of Authenticity, is the coin a good investment at $75? Only if, after a reasonable holding period, a willing buyer can be found at more than $75. The implications of that statement will be discussed in the "liquidity" section below.

Getting the best price may involve comparison shopping, or some bargaining with the dealer. It also requires knowing the total transaction costs involved with a particular item. As in the securities field, some art and collectibles dealers charge less upfront, but commit investors to annual "portfolio management fees" which can be quite expensive. With relatively illiquid items such as art and collectibles there rarely is much real "management" going on, anyway. And will the dealer charge a commission on resale? If, as in the *Solomon Trading* case, the combination of markups and commissions requires unlikely upward market movements in order to break even, the item is overpriced as an investment. Ask dealers to explain their pricing structure, and look for dealers who do so without your asking. For example, Goldline International of Santa Monica, California, places the following disclosure statement in the brochure sent to customers before they make any purchases:

> There is a price differential or "spread" between our selling price and our buy-back price. A typical spread on bullion coins is approximately 2% to 6%, and about 27% to 30% on rare coins. If Goldline's ask/sell price is $500, then Goldline's bid/buy price is $365, less a 1% liquidation/delivery commission ($500 x 73% - 1% = $365). Goldline's minimum buy/sell/liquidation/delivery commission is currently $15/trade. To earn a profit upon re-

sale to us, your coins or bullion must appreciate suffi-
ciently to overcome this price differential.

This is a very candid explanation of the perils of collectibles investing.

Past Appreciation Statistics

Some art and collectibles are pitched to investors through use
of market price data indicating that the items have appreciated, or can be expected to appreciate, in value. The source
and reliability of such data are quite important to its credibil-
ity. In addition, dealers should avoid misleading use of past
appreciation statistics by explaining any extraordinary events
which may skew the figures.

Here's an example. For many years, rare coins were the
highest performers in an annual survey conducted by Salomon
Brothers, the Wall Street investment bankers. In 10-year and 20-
year studies, rare coins increased in value more than Chinese
porcelain, rare stamps, stocks, real estate, and various other categories of investments tracked by Salomon Brothers. Thousands
of investors relied upon reprints of these studies to invest in rare
coins. Unfortunately, Salomon's figures were useless without a
thorough knowledge of the methodology used to create them.
As it turned out, the coins appraised every year were quite eso-
teric and nothing like the types of coins commonly marketed to
investors. In addition, price guides, such as the *Coin Dealer
Newsletter*, which were used by Salomon, were themselves
skewed by steadily more conservative grading interpretations,
which resulted in a phenomenon which Scott Travers, a leading
writer on numismatic investing, described as follows:

> Grading standards are fair stricter now than they were in
> the early days of the Salomon survey. In view of this, the
> "apples" of bygone years really may be lesser-grade "or-
> anges" by today's more stringent yardstick.

And Salomon also did not remind investors that the apparent consistent increases in rare coin prices hid some major market crashes in particular years and that the prices of gold and silver bullion had increased many times during the life of the survey, an increase which was tied to the world metals markets and which was highly unlikely to recur. As a result, the FTC targeted the Salomon survey in its "Consumer Alert" on rare coins:

> Dishonest dealers often mislead buyers by quoting appreciation rates for rare coins from an index formerly compiled each year by Salomon Brothers, a New York investment bank. These quotes show appreciation of 12 percent to 25 percent a year. However, the Salomon index was based on a list of 20 very rare coins, while the coins sold by dishonest dealers are more common coins that are not likely to appreciate at the same rate, if at all. However, almost all dealers, legitimate and dishonest alike, have used the Salomon quotes. . . . Remember, there is no guarantee that any coin will appreciate in value.

In the *Solomon Trading* case discussed on page 52, the art dealer (who was not affiliated in any way with Salomon Brothers) used similarly misleading "performance charts" that supported its salesmen's statements that when Erté prints were released to the public, "the price normally goes up generally anywhere from 23 to 30 percent . . . 10 out of 10 times."

Another problem in tracking the history of art and collectibles market prices is the extreme thinness of those markets at particular moments. As particular genres are promoted at different times, and cash enters or leaves the markets, prices react, and not always predictably. Therefore, the market trends from prior years are not immediately relevant to present or future price rises. And many collectibles have no organized "secondary market" at all, meaning that increased retail prices do not translate to increased wholesale or resale prices.

I am very skeptical of any art and collectible dealer that uses rosy past appreciation statistics as the core of its marketing pitch. These markets are simply too unpredictable, and the items themselves too illiquid, to rely heavily on past performance to predict the future. Also, as an investor you must ask whether the items tracked by these figures are exactly the types of items you are being offered. It is not enough to sell a living artist's works at a high premium because other artists' works have appreciated in value upon their deaths. Look for honest discussions of past appreciation such as given by U.S. Tangible Investment Corporation of Dallas on the back of its customer invoices:

> Various graphs and charts are available as to the performance of coins. The data and basis of those reports must be carefully studied to determine whether the document reflects the performance of the type of coins purchased by the potential investor.
>
> Investment in coins is generally considered a long-term investment, that is, the purchaser must typically hold the coins for several years to have a return of his investment. There is no guarantee that the simple holding of a coin for any period will result in appreciation, as interest in particular series, type, metal, mintage or date may change over the period.

Liquidity

Investors in art and collectibles are often confused when it comes to liquidity. Depending again on the type of item, art and collectible items can be extremely *illiquid*. The importance of that fact to a prospective investor in such items cannot be overstated, and many court cases have arisen over misrepresentations in this area. I ask myself five questions when it comes to liquidity of investment art and collectibles: (1) If I am quoted a market value for an item, is there a willing buyer at that price? (2) Who is that buyer and can I reach him or her? (3) Is that buyer financially able to buy the item at the price? (4) What are the transaction costs involved in selling to that buyer? (5) What is the turn-around time? These questions, in turn, raise a host of other questions, and getting answers is crucial to proper investor education.

Put very simply, no market price valuation is meaningful to an investor unless there is a willing buyer at that price. It is in the very nature of most art and collectible items that they are difficult to sell. Only precious metals have an "exchange" comparable to that which exists for common stocks. Rare coins have an active marketplace consisting of dealers connected by computer networks and meeting face-to-face at shows throughout the country. But much of the lure of art and collectibles comes from their uniqueness or rarity, *i.e.*, the fact that what we're buying isn't so common that it is sold by the thousands every day. Investors in such items pay a big price for that. Even relatively common items are sometimes illiquid when dealers lack cash and/or do not need inventory. A perfect example is post-1940 U.S. postage stamps. I have a nice collection of three-, four-, five-, and six-cent commemorative and regular issue stamps from the period 1940–1975 in full mint sheets. But while the catalogue value of, say, a mint 1953 three-cent General Patton stamp (Scott #1026) may be eight or nine cents, I can't sell my 50-stamp full sheet for 50 times nine cents, *i.e.*, $4.50. In fact, I'd be very happy to sell it at $1.50, the *face value* of the stamps. There aren't enough buyers to absorb the plentiful supply of these stamps, making the catalogue values relatively useless.

A recent article in a popular stamp trade publication discussed how many people who inherit collections from their relatives derive totally unrealistic estimates of the value of these inheritances by looking at catalogues. This is far less true with rare coins, which, no matter how common, nevertheless have published buy prices from reputable dealers that reflect the strength of the rare coin market. But it can be very much the case with art. Another personal example. I have a lovely painting by a popular artist, and every New York gallery I've called tells me how great my painting is, and that it is worth at least 10 percent more than I paid four years ago. But none wants to handle it for me. So what is my painting actually worth? Nothing, until there is a willing buyer.

Investors must be particularly concerned with collectible items that have little to no intrinsic value, but which carry large premiums because of their perceived rarity. Rarity is double-edged. All else being equal, true rarities will have a broader resale market than more common examples of similar items. The 1893-S Morgan Dollar is considerably more marketable than the 1881-S, because far fewer exist. Unlike my stamps and my painting, a true rarity has value to enough people that willing buyers can be found easily. But what will these willing buyers pay? The true rarity carries a different liquidity problem for the investor. It must sell at a premium, because the investor paid a premium to purchase it. Therefore, it cannot be sold to just any willing buyer. It must be offered to the right buyer who will pay its full value. This takes time and adds a certain illiquidity to the item.

An extreme example would be the 11 Kennedy half dollars purchased at the Jackie Onassis auction for $8,645 (including the 15 percent buyer's fee). These coins have a retail value of approximately $10, and Sotheby's estimated them at $200–$300. Are these coins liquid at $8,645? I would say absolutely not. The provenance of these coins, combined with their depiction of President Kennedy, caused the buyer to pay a huge premium. Of course, at the auction there was at least one underbidder at the next lower bidding increment, and probably many others who bid more than $10. Somehow Sotheby's found these people, but how would the present owner of these coins do so? Even auctioning the coins again at Sotheby's would not work. The atmosphere of the Onassis auction was one of near-hysteria, and it will not be duplicated in any resale of individual portions of her property. It is inconceivable to me that Onassis's Kennedy halves would sell for over $8,000 again.

Recall the $75 Winnie the Pooh "coin" I discussed earlier in this chapter. To be a good investment, the medallion must be marketable within a reasonable period of time at a higher price. So before buying this medallion from Disney, an investor might ask, who will ever pay me more than $75 for this? Probably not a coin dealer, because the item isn't a coin, and a coin dealer is unlikely to accept that so large a premium should attach to a contemporary piece. The dealer would pay intrinsic (silver) value, maybe even a little less to cover the cost of handling. Disney? Disney does not make a two-way market in its collectibles. An antique or collectibles dealer? The truth is that there's no "secondary market" in this type of item, and if Disney is fortunate enough to sell all 3,000 Pooh "coins" from its catalogue, the buyers will never know if they can get more than the intrinsic value on resale.

Let's assume we have an item for which a resale market exists and can be identified, and there is some general agreement about market value. Is the item liquid at the market price? Certainly, if the buyer has ready cash for immediate purchase and there are no transaction costs. Here's an example. I called Christie's recently about selling some old Leica camera equipment. Christie's telephoned me with an estimate of £500–£700 for the material, which they later confirmed in writing. But can I sell my camera equipment at that price now? Possibly, but Christie's was not offering to buy it. Christie's was simply offering to accept the equipment for consignment to one of its photography sales to take place in London later in the year. No guarantees were made, and the equipment could sell for less, without even taking into account the commissions Christie's would take on the sale and my costs in getting the items to London. As we will see later, finding a dealer to pay cash for an art or collectible item is difficult, even where the item has a recognized value. For our purposes in this chapter, remember that liquidity involves a realistic assessment of how long an investor must wait to find someone willing to pay market value when it is time to sell.

The final point about liquidity relates to the mechanics of sale: transaction costs and turn-around time. Even relatively liquid items such as shares of IBM common stock cannot be sold instantaneously with no transaction costs, unless one has a seat on the New York Stock Exchange. But stock is considerably more liquid than art or collectibles. If I sold some shares in a mutual fund today, my broker will confirm the trade within the hour, but I will receive a check for the proceeds—minus five percent commission—five days from now. I could shave some time off that turn-around time, and perhaps something off the commission too, but I've chosen to deal through a particular broker that I'm very comfortable with. When selling investment art or collectibles, commissions and turn-around times can be astonishing, depending upon how and through whom you sell.

I've explained how catalogues may not reflect the actual market price of art and collectibles. But lack of liquidity also makes dealer appraisals and "portfolio updates" suspect, unless the dealer is actually offering to buy at the prices given. Auction estimates must likewise be read with some skepticism when the proposed auction is months away. Moreover, investors must understand that there are transaction costs involved with selling their art and collectibles, such as dealer or auctioneer commissions. Liquidity at a certain price is only relevant if that price is *net* of these transaction costs.

A candid discussion of liquidity issues is found in USTIC's customer invoice disclosures:

> The degree of liquidity for PCGS or NGC or any other service's certified coins will vary according to general market conditions and the particular coin involved. For some coins there may be no active market at certain points in time. Although at times the sight-unseen market for coins is strong and offers instant cash, there is no guarantee this system will continue in the future. Further, on many rare and esoteric coins, sight-unseen dealer bids usually reflect only a portion of what the coin is worth. Esoteric and unique rare coins may have limited buyers available when your decision to sell the coin is made, thus the marketing time to maximize the coin's potential can be longer than for more common coins.

Buybacks/Portfolio "Updates"

Some dealers advertise buyback policies, *i.e.,* commitments to repurchase any item they sell on certain terms and conditions. These policies can demonstrate the dealer's faith in its goods, and they can give investors confidence that a two-way market exists in the items they are purchasing. However, buyback policies require some skepticism. When the buyback policy is joined by a policy of providing periodic portfolio updates, you must ask yourself (and the dealer) certain questions.

First, what do the updates/buyback prices mean? Dealers like to use "replacement value" in their updates. That is, the update tells the investor what he or she would have to pay to buy the item at retail that particular day. *Replacement value is not what the dealer would pay you for your item.* The difference between the dealer's "ask" and "bid" depends upon a lot of things, and it is roughly the same as the difference between wholesale and retail described above. It can be substantial. For most art or collectible items, a 20 percent increase in replacement value still means you would suffer a loss if you sold. Without some explanation, replacement value is not an accurate measure of an item's appreciation.

Second, does the dealer have the reserves necessary to finance its buybacks? A buyback commitment is only as strong as the person giving it. Even where the dealer only offers to pay wholesale value, the costs of inventorying an indefinite—and potentially unlimited—amount of material are immense. As the court noted in *FTC v. Security Rare Coin & Bullion Corp.*:

> In order to allay concerns about investing in rare coins, defendants represented to consumers that they maintained a buyback policy, whereby Security would buy back coins from its customers at a discount off the company's prevailing sales prices.
> . . . Defendants did not maintain a reserve of funds to satisfy buy-back requests. If only 10% of defendants' customers had sought to take advantage of the buy-back, defendants would have had insufficient funds to satisfy their requests.

Of course, we know that our banks could not satisfy more than a small fraction of their depositors closing their accounts all at once. However, a dealer in investment art and collectibles must be able to back up a buyback guarantee. Investments, by definition, will peak at certain times, and when selling any genre of art or collectible, the entire genre is likely to peak together. Look for firms which offer to provide audited financial information about themselves before you buy, and ask them to explain how they manage buying back the items they sell.

Third, where buybacks are promised at *more* than the wholesale value, the red flags should be up. Some honest retailers will offer their clients more for art and collectible items than will other dealers because they are more familiar with the items being offered. Offers from a dealer who has actually handled an item will generally be higher than those from dealers who are basing their offers on photographs or telephone descriptions. However, there is always a built-in incentive for retail investment firms to offer clients more than fair market value for their portfolios, to make clients believe that they have profited and to encourage more purchases. But that begins to look like a Ponzi scheme, where yesterday's investors are paid back with today's investors' capital. A rare coin dealer in Southern California provided customers with buyback prices every month and offered an additional 18 percent premium over those prices if the customer waited 30 days for payment. Such a premium is totally unjustified and represented a blatant effort to convince customers that the market was rising so fast that they really should not sell at all.

Fourth, when investors want to cash in, dealers often try to persuade them to shift their "paper" profits into additional purchases. Additional trades result in more profit to the dealer and no real benefit to the investor (and maybe some tax liability). Art and collectibles salespeople can "churn" accounts just like sellers of stocks and bonds.

Dealers as Fiduciaries

Fiduciaries are professionals who owe a special duty of care to their clients, such that they are absolutely liable for any errors or omissions, whether intentional or not. Generally, with investors a fiduciary relationship arises only where the law requires one (such as in the case of trustees), or where the client reasonably believes that the professional is acting primarily in the client's interest and not his own.

Generally speaking, art and collectibles dealers are not fiduciaries of their customers, and that was the finding in *Mechigian v. Art Capital Corp.*, 612 F.Supp. 1421 (S.D.N.Y. 1985), a New York case. Dealers make retail sales of goods to customers in order to earn a profit and do not act primarily for the benefit of their customers, even investors. However, a retail art and collectibles dealer has far more influence over an investor's decision-making and ultimate success than does a stockbroker or other investment advisor. Stocks are priced by an independent, regulated marketplace, and investors have access to independently prepared reports and other documents prior to investing. Those who invest in art and collectibles, however, often find that the dealer both selects and prices the investment vehicle and is solely responsible for disclosing the risks. Though not a fiduciary, the dealer who markets art or collectibles as investments has more responsibility than most other sellers of investments. In some cases, this could rise to the level of a fiduciary relationship.

While no reported case in the major art market states has found that retail art dealers are fiduciaries of their customers, it seems clear that dealers who take items on consignment from investors or collectors are responsible in a fiduciary capacity for loss of such items as well as for the consignor's share of the proceeds once the items are sold. In the case of *Edwards v. Horsemen's Sales Corp.*, 560 N.Y.S. 2d 165 (1989), the New York Supreme Court held that proceeds of an auction sale were held in trust for the consignor and that the principals of an auction house were personally liable for paying them over to the consignor. And in *Cristallina v. Christie's*, 117 A.D.2d 284, 502 N.Y.S. 2d 165 (1st Dep't 1986), a case which will be discussed in more detail in Chapter 8, a New York court held that Christie's acted in a fiduciary capacity toward a major consignor because its "influence and control" extended to all aspects of the transaction, to the point that decisions crucial to the consignor's financial interest were being made by Christie's and not by the consignor itself.

Telephone or Television Solicitations

Art and collectibles are often marketed over the telephone or on television. Often, telemarketing campaigns are intended for investors, although there are major retailers and cable television shopping networks who sell to collectors. When buying over the telephone some of the risks I've been discussing in this chapter may be greater because you don't actually see the item in person before you buy, and telephone salespeople can be quite deceptive regarding quality, pricing, and liquidity. However, special protective rules and regulations apply to telephone sales as a result of recent congressional and FTC action.

On August 16, 1994, President Clinton signed into law the Telemarketing and Consumer Fraud and Abuse Prevention Act, 15 U.S.C. §6101 *et seq.,* directing the FTC to issue rules prohibiting deceptive and abusive telemarketing acts and practices. The Act authorized the FTC to issue regulations requiring telemarketers to make appropriate disclosures about the nature and price of the goods or services being sold.

The FTC's Telemarketing Sales Rule took effect on January 1, 1996. "Telemarketing" is defined as any plan, program, or campaign which is conducted to induce payment for goods and services by use of more than one interstate telephone call. Mail order dealers persuaded the FTC to exclude from this definition telephone calls initiated by customers responding to postcards, brochures, and advertisements. However, a major exception exists in the case of "investment opportunities," defined as anything offered for sale, sold, or traded based on express or implied representations about income, profit, or appreciation. In cases involving investment opportunities, even incoming calls by customers are covered by the Rule.

Here are some examples. A firm which solicits the sale of art prints or rare coins through "cold" calls is clearly covered. However, what about the companies who advertise "limited edition" or "collectible" items such as dolls, plates, and commemorative coins and medals in the Sunday magazine sections of newspapers? When there is a mention of how prior items in a particular series have appreciated in value over time, or any hint that demand for a particular item will increase in the future, the offer would probably be considered telemarketing. However, when only the mintage is given, or the words "limited edition" are used several times, that should not cross the line into an implied representation about income, profit, or appreciation.

All sales by telemarketers are subject to certain requirements under the Telemarketing Act. First, before consummating the sale, the seller must affirmatively disclose to the buyer the number of items sold, the purchase price, and the seller's refund/exchange/buyback policy. The dealer is not *required* to have such a policy, but if it does, disclosure must be made. Second, dealers must avoid misrepresenting material facts about the items being sold. As we've seen, material misrepresentations are unlawful anyway. But as we will see in Chapters 10 and 11, through the Telemarketing Act and the Telemarketing Sales Rule, Congress and the FTC enhanced the remedies available to victims of telemarketing fraud, making the Rule a major improvement in consumer protection.

Are Art or Collectible Items Securities?

Because so many people invest in art and collectibles as part of an overall portfolio including stocks, bonds, and other securities, the question has arisen whether art and collectibles dealers have the same responsibilities as sellers of securities. This question has appeared in several court cases and is still unresolved.

The leading definition of "security" comes from the U.S. Supreme Court's decision in *SEC v. W.J. Howey Co.*, 328 U.S. 293 (1946). In *Howey*, the Court held that a transaction constitutes a sale of securities if it "involves an investment of money in a common enterprise with profits to come solely from the efforts of others." *Howey, supra*, 328 U.S. at 301. This has been interpreted by lower federal courts as a requirement that the success or failure of the investment depends upon the efforts of others besides the investors. *SEC v. Glenn W. Turner Enterprises, Inc.*, 474 F.2d 476, 482 (9th Cir.), *cert. denied*, 414 U.S. 821 (1973). Since *Howey*, a federal appeals court in California has stated that when investors buy bullion coins, or buy rare coins in a one-shot retail transaction, their profits come entirely from fluctuations in the coin market that are out of the dealer's control. *SEC v. Belmont Reid & Co., Inc.,* 794 F.2d 1388 (9th Cir. 1986) held that gold bullion coins were not securities because the market value was determined independently of the dealer. In *SEC v. Brigadoon Scotch Distributors, Ltd.,* 388 F.Supp. 1288 (S.D.N.Y. 1975), however, a New York federal district judge found that First Coin Rarities, which also sold rare coins, was selling securities:

> [I]t is significant that FCR's advertising brochure . . . consistently described the collection of rare coins as an "investment." Comparisons of gains in the stock market with returns from coins, analysis of coin appreciation and similar investment information run in a constant and main stream throughout FCR's sales pitch. The placement of advertisements in airline magazines and medical journals rather than in numismatic periodicals bolsters the view that the thrust of FCR's efforts are directed at an investing, rather than a coin-collecting, public.

Id. at 1291. The court emphasized the fact that half of FCR's sales were of coins selected for customers by FCR itself:

> This fact alone persuades us that the third aspect of the Howey test, that is, the dependence of the investor on the expertise of the seller to produce the expected profit, is present here. Coins do not appreciate at the same rate and accordingly their selection is the most crucial factor in determining how much profit an investor in coins will make. . . . And the presence of the package of investment advice and information referred to above of course only supports our finding.

SEC v. Brigadoon, supra, 388 F. Supp. at 1293. Under the *Brigadoon* approach, nearly all art or collectibles dealers who sell primarily to investors will be deemed to be selling securities. Other federal district courts have rejected *Brigadoon* and found that rare coins are not securities. The SEC, when asked, has chosen a middle path by refusing to issue "no-action" letters—statements that certain types of transactions are not sales of securities—to three rare coin and collectibles dealers, while never actually prosecuting such dealers for failing to register. New York State, however, recently prosecuted a rare coin dealer for failing to register as a broker-dealer under New York State's securities law, the Martin Act.

The ramifications of art and collectibles being the legal equivalent of securities is beyond the scope of this book, and many of the key concepts of securities fraud litigation—misrepresentations, reliance, causation—have already been discussed earlier in this chapter. I don't think that the legal authorities so far give any clear picture on this point, and it simply remains one possible argument for investors to raise.

Summary

If you are ready to buy art or collectibles as an investment, keep the following in mind:

- what sounds too good to be true probably isn't
- understand the concept of liquidity and do not buy illiquid items unless you don't expect to ever have to sell quickly
- understand the retail markups by learning exactly what you would get if you sold the item the day after purchase
- carefully review all representations relating to grade, condition, and rarity, and make sure they are based on industry-wide standards, or are correlated to industry-wide standards
- look for balanced presentations regarding past performance statistics, understanding that in every market there are ups and downs
- find out the dealer's refund and repurchase policy and, remembering that these policies are only as strong as the dealer itself, ask for financial information about the dealer
- don't do business with dealers that are reluctant to give you the information you need to make a purchase

6

Selling Art or Collectibles through Dealers

Many collectors and investors choose to sell art or collectibles through a dealer rather than an auction house. There are various reasons for this, including prior relationship with the dealer, the prospect of prompt sale and settlement, and a dealer's special ability to find buyers of rare or unusual pieces. In choosing a dealer through whom to sell, consider such factors as years in business, reputation, special expertise with the type of item, and professional affiliations. If the item is sizable, by all means interview the dealer and ask questions. And keep in mind the principles discussed below.

The Buyer as Seller—Warranties

If a sale is outright, a simple contract or bill of sale is sufficient to document the sale. As a non-dealer, you will not be bound to many of the legal rules and regulations discussed in Chapters 2 and 3 for retail sales by dealers. For example, you will not make implied warranties of merchantability, because under the UCC such warranties are only implied into sales by "merchants in the particular goods." This fact also makes disclaimer of warranties easier for collector-sellers than it is for dealers. In addition, nondealers ordinarily are not required to collect or pay sales or use taxes in connection with their sales of art or collectibles because they are considered "occasional sellers" for tax purposes. Finally, a dealer will be held to have the same or superior knowledge of the field compared to a non-dealer, such that he cannot claim to have been deceived by misleading statements regarding an item.

However, the basic rules of contract law which govern all sales of goods will still apply. This was made clear in the case of *Feigen & Co. v. Weil*, in which Richard Feigen, a prominent New York art dealer, purchased a drawing from an art collector for $100,000, and resold it to a client for $165,000, believing it to be by Matisse. When the client showed the drawing to another gallery, the gallery checked with the Matisse estate and discovered that the drawing was a forgery. Feigen immediately refunded the client's $165,000, but had to sue the collector to recover his $100,000. The collector argued that Feigen, as a dealer, could have checked with the Matisse estate himself before buying the drawing, and therefore Feigen should bear the risk of a "mutual mistake" regarding authenticity. The court disagreed and ruled in Feigen's favor, stating that a mutual mistake in the sale of art is, indeed, just that, regardless of whether the injured buyer happens to be the dealer rather than the collector.

Consignments to Dealers— Terms and Conditions

Dealers do not usually buy art or collectible items outright. Rather, they agree to take them on consignment. Consignment is the legal term for transferring to another person the right to sell one's property. In the case of art or collectibles dealers, a consignment agreement provides that the dealer will be paid a commission for finding a buyer and concluding a sale of the property. The terms and conditions of consignment agreements are quite important, and as with the contract of sale itself, they should be negotiated carefully and put in writing.

The first term is whether the consignment is what attorneys call an "exclusive right to sell." In other words, is the dealer the only person who may sell the item during the period of the consignment, or do you reserve rights to sell the item yourself or through another dealer? Many dealers will not take consignments without exclusive rights because they fear making extensive efforts to sell only to learn that another dealer (or the owner) sold the item and no commission is due them.

The next term is the length of the consignment. Sellers want results, and it is fair to limit the length of time that a particular dealer has to survey its clients and promote the item. On the other hand, works of art or rare collectibles often do not find their optimum buyer quickly, and they will not achieve their best prices if the seller appears too anxious. Take the dealer's advice and be clear on your own financial needs. If the desired price is not obtained within the agreed period of time, the consignment is terminated. In some consignments, the item is immediately returned to the owner. In others, the dealer is required to purchase the item at a pre-agreed price. The latter works better for collectors who do not want the property back and are willing to accept a little less in order to have a sale.

Of course, the commission rate is also a crucial term. Commissions vary with the customs and mechanics of different markets. The commission on sales of fine art paintings may be considerably higher than that of rare coins. In some cases, the collector or investor will set a desired price and will award the dealer a higher commission as an incentive if he or she is able to sell the item for a higher price. Conversely, if the dealer receives an offer lower than the desired price, the owner might agree to it on condition that the dealer reduce his or her commission.

One crucial aspect of consigning property to a dealer is protection against the "entruster" rule and claims by the dealer's other creditors. As discussed in Chapter 4 in the context of buying art or collectibles, the "entruster rule" allows dealers to pass good title to consigned goods, regardless of whether the dealer has complied with the terms of the consignment. For example, a collector may consign paintings to a dealer based upon the dealer's agreement to pay the collector 50 percent of the sale price within 30 days of any sale. If the dealer sells a painting and does not pay, the collector can no longer demand return of the painting, has no rights whatsoever against the buyer of the painting, and is left only with a claim against the dealer.

The Entruster Rule—Protecting Yourself

In addition to the risk of a dealer passing title to consigned goods under the entruster rule, there is also the risk that consigned goods will be seized to satisfy claims by the dealer's secured creditors, which can include everyone from the IRS to another consignor. Dealers who rely on bank financing generally give the lender a security interest in their office fixtures, accounts receivable, and inventory. Because a dealer's inventory includes consigned goods, should the dealer default on his loan payments, the bank might well be able to seize property on consignment to sell in order to satisfy the debt.

Probably the most interesting case I have come across in this area involved a Minneapolis rare coin dealer, who was placed into receivership after a lawsuit by the FTC and subsequently filed for bankruptcy. The federal district court judge appointed me as the receiver for the dealer, and it was my job to investigate claims to hundreds of rare coins the company held as inventory. It turned out that many of company's customers were investors, and the company offered them commission-free sales of their coins. Unfortunately, the company rarely paid promptly after the sales. During my investigations, I learned that a substantial number of coins consigned by customers had been sold and the customers were not even notified, much less paid. Others were not sold, but were held as inventory for sale, and the company borrowed against them and actually shipped them to the bank until the loans were paid off. Even after the bank was paid and it released the coins, as court-appointed receiver my rights to the consigned coins were superior to those of the customers, and this carried through when a bankruptcy trustee took over for me. The customers had nothing other than a claim for return of their purchase price. Instead of getting their coins back, they got pennies on the dollar.

I'm often asked for advice on how art and collectibles consignors can protect their property in such situations. This is a complicated question, but remembering some simple rules will help avoid trouble. First, protecting yourself requires some degree of cooperation from the dealer. The very wording of your agreement may determine whether the deal is determined to be a true consignment (where the dealer doesn't own the property) or a secured sale (where title passes, subject to your security interest). In addition, to give notice of the consignment to the dealer's subsequent creditors, you may need to file a UCC-1 financing statement (one notice works against all subsequent creditors), and that must be signed by the dealer. Notice to *prior* creditors such as the dealer's bank requires that the dealer tells you who those creditors are. The best—usually the only—time to expect such cooperation is before the property is delivered to the dealer, so make these points part of your negotiations up front.

Second, spend the time and money to prepare a written consignment agreement rather than scribble something on a "receipt" or other generic document. That way, you'll say what you need to say, and everyone (including a court or government attorney) can see that the consignment is legally effective. Most "memo" agreements I've seen dealers use simply wouldn't stand up in court to protect the consignor. State laws resolve any doubts in favor of the consignee's creditors (*i.e.*, against the consignor) when the consignee is a dealer. The law disregards such phrases as "on consignment" or "on memorandum," or the commonly used "title does not pass until payment in full" when considering claims of prior creditors or the government.

Third, beware of the dealer commingling your property with his or her other inventory. For unique works of art this isn't a concern. But when your collection of 100 Morgan silver dollars ends up in inventory along with someone else's, maintaining title and/or security in your material becomes more complicated. The law provides only an imperfect solution here, but you can still protect yourself in most cases.

Fourth, get good information about the consignee. A UCC search will give you a printout of all the consignee's prior secured creditors at a minimal cost, and I recommend this before any major consignment. Staying alert to the dealer's financial difficulties is also crucial. Although I tell clients to make security arrangements before turning over the coins, "better late than never" applies, too.

7

Miscellaneous Aspects of Buying Art or Collectibles

This chapter discusses certain aspects of buying art and collectibles which are important but are not treated with the same detail as the others. For most buyers and sellers, these should not be a problem, but I wanted to alert the reader to their implications.

Risk of Loss When Buying through the Mail

Whether buying retail or at auction, many art and collectibles are received by mail or courier shipment from their source. Ordinarily, sellers require payment in full before shipping, and therefore the buyer must be concerned about receiving items intact and unharmed in transit. Risk of loss during shipment may be allocated between buyer and seller, and before making a mail order or auction purchase, buyers should know where the risk lies in the particular transaction. Most dealers and auction houses are insured for losses occurring during shipment to or from their places of business, and it is common for them to accept the risk of loss.

However, it is not necessarily the case that a dealer or auctioneer's insurance will pay the full retail price of an item lost, stolen, or damaged during shipment. Some insurance policies cover only fair market value, or even 80 percent of fair market value. Unless a policy expressly defines fair market value to include retail price, the insurer's payment may be based only on the item's *wholesale* value, which is substantially less than most retail buyers pay. Moreover, where items are damaged and are restorable, the insurer may pay only the restoration costs. In these situations, collectors are legitimately concerned about whether restoration adequately restores an item's pre-damage value, or whether the item should be declared a total loss. Of course, reputable dealers will often make up any difference between the insurance proceeds and the purchase price, but I still see many purchase invoices which do not commit the dealer to do this, or expressly limit loss recoveries to actual insurance proceeds paid. Where items of substantial value are involved, it is worth asking the dealer about risk of loss and insurance and getting a copy of the dealer's insurance policy.

Return Privileges

Most art and collectibles dealers will permit a customer to change his or her mind about a purchase within a reasonable time, and they will accept return of the item(s) for a full refund with no questions asked. Some, however, accept returns only where authenticity is in question, and some do not accept returns for any reason. While dealers should not have to accept returns of items whose value has decreased sharply since the time of purchase, most art and collectible items are not so volatile, and a return privilege is a sign that the dealer stands behind his or her product.

Return periods are usually measured from the date the buyer receives delivery and should allow enough time to get a second opinion on the item (*i.e.,* three business days). However, be sure to understand the terms and conditions that apply to returns. For example, with rare coins, dealers may require that the coins be returned in their original packaging.

Nobody buys art or collectibles with the intent to return them. But it is prudent to know the dealer's return policy before making a purchase. The Telemarketing Act requires mail order dealers to disclose their return policies, but it does not require them to allow returns (only to disclose whether they do or not).

Illegal Art or Collectibles

Believe it or not, some art and collectible items are illegal to own, or restricted in their importation and sale. A great example of the former is playing out in a federal court in New York City as I'm writing this. A British rare coin dealer was arrested in a sting operation for trying to sell an undercover Secret Service agent a U.S. 1933 $20 gold piece. In March 1933, President Franklin Roosevelt outlawed private ownership of gold except for "rare and unusual coins" held by collectors. The 1933 $20 gold pieces that had already been minted for circulation that year were melted down and never issued. However, prior to Roosevelt's order, apparently a few examples of the coin had left the Mint in an unknown way. Even though the ban on gold ownership has long since been repealed, the government's position ever since 1933 has been that those coins are subject to confiscation without compensation. Needless to say, the coin is quite rare today, although not "rare and unusual" by 1933's standards. Many numismatic scholars say that examples of the coin left quite legally when individuals approached Mint personnel and traded in older $20 gold pieces on a one-to-one basis, and they are appalled that the government could make it illegal to own a U.S. legal tender coin.

Among other "illegal" pieces are artworks which too closely resemble U.S. currency (the talented artist J.S.G. Boggs has made a career out of painting reproductions of U.S. paper money and feuding with the Secret Service over his First Amendment right to do so), or which contain images classified as "child pornography" under state statutes. General obscenity laws have resulted in the closing of critically acclaimed exhibitions by Robert Mapplethorpe. And each year Congress considers legislation to ban artwork which desecrates the U.S. flag or subjects it to ridicule. A constitutional amendment may eventually be passed to protect the flag. The pros and cons of art and the First Amendment are a book in themselves.

Some types of collectibles also are illegal to sell. A federal law entitled the Hobby Protection Act, 15 U.S.C. §§2101–06, prohibits the sale of replica coins or political memorabilia unless the word "COPY" is conspicuously placed on one side of the item. Regulations prescribe the size and location of the "COPY" notice, and it is practically impossible to mistake a properly marked replica item for the genuine article (which, of course, is the purpose of the Act). Congress feared that the proliferation of collectibles in the 1970s would encourage counterfeiters, and the Hobby Protection Act provides some limited protection. Replicas of collectible items may also be restricted by federal trademark and unfair competition statutes, most notably the Lanham Act, 15 U.S.C. §1125(a), and equivalent state laws.

Copyright

Buyers of original works of art sometimes think they are acquiring all rights to the works, including the right to reproduce them in other forms. Prior to 1976, this was partly true, in that copyright to an original work of art was transferred along with title to the work in the absence of a written agreement reserving copyright to the seller. The Copyright Act of 1976 reversed this presumption—copyright is not transferred unless a written agreement so provides. So although you may *own* a painting or sculpture, you may not *reproduce* its copyrighted image without the permission of the copyright owner, usually the artist. The copyright owner may, however, make reproductions in the same or other media. I own a painting which was made into a series of serigraphs after I bought it. Lithographs and posters are often made of popular works of art. Only the copyright owner, or someone licensed by the copyright owner, has the right to make such reproductions. Licenses usually require paying the copyright owner a royalty based upon the nature and scope of the intended use.

Whether or not a particular work of art is protected by copyright is beyond the scope of this book, although if it carries a copyright notice—the © symbol followed by the artist's name and the date of publication—chances are it is copyrighted. But the converse is not true—items which do not bear a copyright notice may still be copyrighted. Do not be fooled by a museum's use of artwork on brochures or gift shop items such as T-shirts, mugs, and notepads. In some cases the works being reproduced may be in the public domain, but museums also obtain permission from artists for reproducing their works. Moreover, nonprofit educational institutions have greater rights to use copyrighted images than do commercial enterprises.

Consult a copyright attorney if you want to reproduce works of art for commercial purposes. Copyright is the most important property right artists have, and artists are quite vigilant in enforcing their legal rights.

Moral Rights

In addition to restrictions on reproduction rights based on copyright law, the owner of a work of art might be limited in his or her use of that work by an artist's "moral rights." Moral rights, also known by the French term of *droit moral,* include, among other things, artists' rights to regulate how their works are displayed and to protect their works from destruction or mutilation even after ownership of the work itself and/or its copyright are transferred to third parties.

Moral rights are a European invention, and are embodied in international treaties as well as various foreign statutes. In the United States, a moral rights movement resulted in legislation being enacted in several states during the 1980s. These state enactments attempted to balance artists' rights with the property rights held by owners of artwork or of structures in which artwork has been incorporated permanently (such as in the case of murals, mosaics, and certain types of sculptures).

In 1991, the federal Visual Artists' Rights Act (VARA), 17 U.S.C. §§101 *et seq.,* established a nationwide moral rights regime, in the process pre-empting portions of the earlier state enactments. In the case of *Carter v. Helmsley-Spear* in 1994, a federal court in New York applied VARA for the first time, enjoining the owner of a commercial office building from removing an unusual sculpture commissioned by a former tenant who had defaulted on its lease and left the building (the ruling was recently reversed on appeal on other grounds). Other cases have involved a sculpture split in half when its owner decided it took up too much space, a painting displayed next to a museum's fire exit, and a television comedy show which was edited against the wishes of the writer/performer's permission.

Our notions of private property do not easily accept moral rights. Why shouldn't the owner of a sculpture be able to cut it in two if he or she wants to? Of course, moral rights generally apply only to works which are publicly displayed, so presumably sculptures kept in the back yard have less protection than those in the front yard. This, too, seems odd. Moreover, moral rights are personal to the artist, can never be transferred, and do not follow the copyright. This means that even the owner of a work who also owns the copyright cannot do what he or she pleases without potential liability to the artist. The justification for moral rights is the artist's need to protect his or her reputation by making sure works are displayed the way the artist intended them to be. Art collectors must respect this.

Resale Rights

European artists receive royalties for subsequent sales of their art, *i.e.*, for sales following the initial sale made directly by the artist himself or herself. In countries such as France and Germany, such "resale royalties" compensate the artist for appreciating values of art over time. It is believed that artists spending much of their careers in obscurity are not properly paid for earlier works which later trade at huge multiples of their original prices.

California adopted a resale royalty law in the mid-1970s (California Civil Code 986), and it remains the only state in which artists—theoretically, at least—are entitled to a share (five percent) of the proceeds of all sales of their works for their lifetime plus 20 years, regardless of whether the sale is by a gallery or a private collector. The rights are limited in several ways, however. First, they apply only to the sale of "fine art" which is defined as original paintings, sculptures, and drawings. Second, resale rights apply only when the seller lives in California or the sale itself takes place there. Third, sales below $1,000, sales at a loss, and sales by a dealer who bought the item directly from the artist are exempt.

Part Two:
Buying and Selling Art and Collectibles at Auction

Many people think that only the most expensive art and collectibles are sold at public auction. This is untrue, and public auction is a very popular method for buying and selling all types of art and collectibles. However, it is considerably different in many ways from the retail transactions discussed in the prior chapters, so review Chapters 8 and 9 carefully before you decide to buy or sell at auction.

8

Consigning to Auction

Auctioneers bring buyers and sellers together. Beyond that
simple statement lies a multi-billion-dollar industry. Collectors who wish to sell all or part of their collections know
that they will achieve the highest price only by exposing the
items being sold to the maximum number of other collectors.
Where the items are exotic or of only narrow collecting interest, this exposure is even more important, and the seller must
have confidence that what few collectors there are in a particular area will know that his or her property is for sale. Auctioneers serve the function of advertising the prospective sale
of art and collectible property, and managing the business aspects of that sale. A professional auction house acts as warehouse, appraiser, insurer, photographer, researcher, bank,
salesperson, and credit manager for its consignor, in ways that
we will discuss. For the buyers, the auctioneer is authentica-
tor, appraiser, and delivery service. And even these lists don't
do justice to the auctioneer's pivotal role in the art and collectibles industry. The many benefits of public auction explain
the near overwhelming use of that method of sale in the
largest art and collectibles transactions.

Property is consigned to the auction house for sale, usually pursuant to a written consignment agreement. Although the wording of these agreements varies somewhat among auction houses, certain subjects are nearly always covered, and must be considered in working out the business terms of the consignment.

Exclusive Right to Sell

Auction houses require that consignors give them the exclusive right to sell the items being consigned. This means that items cannot be withdrawn from sale by the consignor except as provided by the Consignment Agreement. Ordinarily, there is no right to withdraw at all, and consignors may reclaim their consigned property only if the property fails to meet a reserve bid, or if the consignor buys his or her own property at the sale. The auction house will not undertake the effort of cataloguing and promoting the goods if the consignor has the right to withdraw them or sell them elsewhere.

The flip side, however, is that an auction consignor is locked into the auction process once he or she signs the Consignment Agreement. Keeping in mind that auctions usually take place months after the Agreement is signed, a consignor choosing between selling directly to a dealer and public auction takes a gamble that by the time of the auction circumstances will not have changed to his or her detriment. The art and collectibles market can be very volatile, and today's favorable trends could become extremely unfavorable while your property awaits auction. Personal circumstances can also change to the point where a quicker sale would be advantageous. Despite the contract provisions, auction house staff are human beings and are sensitive to their consignors' needs and desires. In compelling situations, they will agree to allow withdrawal of items even after they have done most of their work, sometimes without charge.

Despite the consignor's binding commitment to the auction house, the auction house usually reserves for itself the right to withdraw items from an auction without the consignor's permission, and without compensation to the consignor. This is rarely done, because no commissions are earned on withdrawn items. However, where there are questions of authenticity, an auction house may withdraw items rather than sell a fake. Another reason auction houses withdraw items is to sell them at "private treaty." Selling through an auction house does not always mean a traditional public auction, and auction houses sometimes act as dealers and make direct sales without catalogues and bidding by the public. Private treaties are appropriate when it is clear who the top buyers will be. Items are offered to these buyers, and a favorable sale is negotiated promptly, without either the expense or possible market risks inherent with auctions.

Timing/Location of Sale

Auction houses hold sales at different times of the year, sometimes in different locations. There are sales traditionally held in certain weeks, such as the Impressionist paintings sales at Sotheby's and Christie's. Other sales are held in conjunction with shows or fairs, when dealers and collectors are in town. Timing can be crucial, not just because the markets in art and collectibles are so volatile, but also because it is best to sell when dealers and collectors can take notice and bid. This argues for placing your goods along with other similar items in sales featuring such items, such as selling Hawaiian stamps in a Hawaiian stamp sale. However, it occasionally happens that too many of a particular type of item in one sale may dilute bidding interest and result in lower prices.

The dominant market for fine art auctions in the United States is New York City, and with few exceptions, Sotheby's and Christie's hold their major sales there. Los Angeles, San Francisco, and Chicago are lesser art auction markets, and the rest of the country is developing slowly. This is likewise the case for rare stamps, which are generally auctioned in New York. For rare coins, major auctions take place nationwide. Leading firms such as Heritage, Stack's, Superior, and Bowers and Merena hold major auctions during fairs such as the Long

Beach Coin and Collectibles Expo and the Florida United Numismatists Convention. The largest rare coin auction of the year is generally held in conjunction with the American Numismatic Association's annual convention, which is held in a different city every year. For some types of art and collectibles, sales should be held outside the United States to reach the greatest number of bidders, and that is usually the case for specialized foreign art, antiquities, stamps, and coins.

Consignors have a limited influence on when and where their property is sold. Of course, consignment deadlines usually pass some months before a sale, so the timing of a consignor's contract determines which sales are still open. Beyond that, auction houses are quite candid when it comes to advising which sales would be best for particular material. The major art and antique auction houses have two tiers of sales, one in the main salesroom and one in a second space, such as Sotheby's "Arcade Auction." Generally, only the top items will be sold in the main sales room, and items of under $5,000 will go to the alternate spaces.

Commissions and Other Charges

For the consignor, the primary cost of selling at auction is the seller's commission, which is a percentage of the "hammer price" (winning bid) of each item. The seller's commission places the auction house's interests right alongside the consignor's, as increasing the hammer prices increases compensation to both. The amount of the seller's commission varies depending upon the type of item and the value of the total consignment. For example, the usual seller's commission in U.S. rare coin sales is 10 to 15 percent of the hammer price of the consignment, while for sales of foreign coins it is 15 percent, and for certain types of art or collectibles it may be as high as 25 percent. However, auction houses are quite competitive with one another when negotiating for major consignments, and as the value of the consignment increases, the commission rate tends to decline, until it reaches two percent or less after the $1 million threshold is passed. Many important collections of art or collectibles are actually sold at a zero percent seller's commission. Negotiating commission rates is beyond the scope of this book, but if you have a major consignment it is worth consulting an expert regarding which auction house(s) will best serve your needs and what commission rates might be available to you.

In addition to the seller's commission, auction houses charge buyers a commission, usually called a buyer's "premium" or "fee," which ranges from 10 to 20 percent depending upon the auction house and the type of item being sold. This is when the auction house recoups its expenses and earns its profit, particularly when the seller's commission has been negotiated down to zero. Buyers at auction should take the buyer's premium into account when they decide how much to bid. Here's an example. You want to bid on a collectible at an auction where a 20 percent buyer's premium is being applied. The most you are willing to pay for it is $10,000, and the estimate is $9,000 to $10,000. Your highest bid should be approximately $8,400, because should that bid be successful your total cost will be $10,080. Consignors also must understand the impact of buyer's premiums on their likely net proceeds from the items they sell. In the previous example, the consignor of the $9,000 to $10,000 collectible might receive only $7,560 for it, based on a 10 percent seller's commission:

Hammer price	$8,400
Total proceeds	$10,080
Buyer's comm'n—$1,680 (20% of hammer)	
Seller's comm'n—$ 840 (10% of hammer)	
Total comm'ns to auction house	$ 2,520
Proceeds to consignor	$ 7,560

Don't let the above example scare you away from auctions, however. For many items, the major auction houses have lower cost "arcade" auctions, in which the auction house's costs are reduced, usually by the absence of a printed catalogue, minimal advertising, and reduced public viewing. Commissions are far lower in such sales.

In addition to commissions, auction houses often require consignors to compensate them for certain additional out-of-pocket costs. One such cost is photography. Whether the auction is of Revolutionary War documents or movie posters, Rembrandts or animation art, the photographs contained in the auction catalogue are very important to mail bidders who cannot view the items personally prior to the sale. Quality photographs help the consignor by inviting more bids, thereby increasing activity on the item and, hopefully, increasing the price realized. Some auction houses use extremely high-quality color photographs for every item, others use photographs only for the most important items, and still others use no photographs at all. Photography costs are substantial, and some—though not all—auction houses will charge a fee of one to two percent of the hammer price to cover those costs. In large consignments, these charges are absorbed by the auction house. In any event, consignors should get an agreement (preferably in writing, as a rider to the consignment agreement) stating which items will be photographed, the size of the photographs, and whether they will appear alongside the item's written description in the catalogue or collectively with others elsewhere in the catalogue.

The second out-of-pocket expense auction houses often try to pass along to consignors is insurance. Major auction houses will insure items against loss or damage from the time they are shipped by the consignor to when the ultimate buyer picks them up after the sale. Make sure of this before you do business with an auction house. In some cases, the insured value is set by the consignor, and in others, the insured value is simply fair market value. The consignment agreement usually provides that in the event of loss, the auction house will assign its rights under the policy to the consignor, in exchange for which the consignor releases the auction house from any liability. If the loss occurs after the sale, but before the buyer has picked up the item, the auction house will deduct its commission from the insurance proceeds before turning them over to the consignor. Consignors are entitled to see the insurance policy which will apply to their property. The usual insurance charge is also one to two percent of the hammer price, depending upon the auction house and the type of item. Some auction houses absorb these costs on every item, others only with large consignments.

Advances

As we have seen, there is generally a long period of time between when goods are consigned and when the consignor is paid for them after sale. As a convenience to consignors, auction houses usually offer consignors advances. Advances are loans, with interest, payable from the proceeds of the sale. Generally, a large consignor can borrow 50 percent or more of the estimated value of the consignment. The major auction houses have separate financing companies which arrange advances, and the amounts can be quite significant. The benefits of taking advances from an auction house are obvious—it puts cash into your pocket long before the auction, and auction houses are among the few people who will loan substantial amounts of money on the security of art and collectible objects. However, the interest rates can be high, although even this is negotiable in very large consignments (I've represented consignors who received interest-free advances from a major auction house). Overall, I don't recommend advances unless the terms are right and there really is a need for cash before the sale.

If you do go ahead with an advance, you will be asked to sign a loan agreement and a security agreement, both of which will be on that auction house's standard printed form and will not (ordinarily) be negotiable. The agreements will authorize the auction house to subtract all amounts due on the loan from the proceeds of sale before paying the balance over to the consignor. They will provide that in the event that the items consigned sell for less than the amount due on the loan, you will promptly make up the difference. Also, they will provide that if the consigned items do not sell, they may be held as collateral by the auction house until the loan is repaid with interest.

Cataloguing

The auction house is responsible for preparing a catalogue describing all the lots in a sale and mailing the catalogue to its list of potential bidders. This is an important function, and how a lot is described in the catalogue can greatly affect the bids received. Keep in mind that many bidders never see the items they bid upon before the sale, and they have only the catalogue descriptions (and photographs, if any) to go on.

Consignment agreements usually provide that the auction house has complete discretion with respect to all aspects of cataloguing. The first of these is lotting, *i.e.,* dividing the consignment into lots for sale. It would not be unusual for a collection of 200 common U.S. and foreign stamps to be divided into fewer than 10 lots, with the bulk of the material being grouped together into large lots. Do not expect that each and every item you consign will be a separate lot. Consignors who are unfamiliar with auction practices sometimes resent this, thinking that their "gems" aren't being properly handled. Remember that the auction house has every reason to want the items to sell for the most possible, and when making lotting decisions the auction house must balance the costs of individually lotting items with the benefits. In the stamp example above, individually lotting a large collection of foreign stamps will probably result in many lots going unsold because bidders simply aren't interested in bidding on them one at a time. It would also lengthen the auction tremendously and increase the auction house's costs for the auction. However, a large lot will sell to a collector or dealer who finds value in the group as a whole, and it will save time and money for the auction house.

A second cataloguing decision about which the auction house has total discretion is lot numbering, meaning the order in which items are auctioned. This isn't as wide open as it may sound. Rare coins are almost always ordered by denomination, and by date within a particular denomination. Large cents come before 20-cent pieces, and before silver dollars. Stamps are usually ordered by Scott catalogue number, U.S. first followed by foreign in alphabetical (by country) order. Art and antiques auctions can be far different, and many experts have theories about where items are best placed in an auction to attract maximum bidding. As a consignor, it is worth knowing whether your item(s) will be sold at seven p.m. on the first day of the auction or at one a.m. on the third day. While mail bidders are just as active in the wee hours, floor bidders often are not.

The actual descriptions of the items are also ultimately in the auction house's sole discretion. For each item, the auction house's own staff, sometimes supplemented by renowned experts in specific fields, prepares a description which may include authenticity, provenance, rarity, condition, and any special attributes or associations pertaining to an item. Here, every nuance can affect bidding. We have seen the legal difference between attributing a work of art to an artist or the "school" of the artist. Likewise, the use of phrases such as "best known" in describing an item might greatly influence bidders on that item. As a consignor, you have some right to know what the auction house plans to say about your property, and auction houses will sometimes (not often) offer to submit proposed lot descriptions to you for review. You may even be able to suggest changes and ask the auction house to add to, subtract from, or modify their descriptions. However, the final say lies with the auction house, whose reputation depends, in part, on the integrity and reliability of its lot descriptions.

In addition to the *content* of the description, consignors occasionally negotiate the *size* of the space given to a particular lot. Regardless of the description itself, items which receive a full page in the catalogue attract more attention than those with only a few lines. This is another area where the dollar value of the item is important.

Consignor's Warranties

The consignment agreement will contain a warranty from the consignor regarding title to the goods being consigned. This warranty enables the auction house, in turn, to warrant title to the ultimate buyer. In New York, the law requires such a warranty, but even without such a law an auction house would be unlikely to accept a consignment where the consignor does not warrant title. The warranty of title consists of assurances that the consignor has sole title and power over the goods, that there are no liens or encumbrances over the goods, and that nobody else must consent to the auction sale of the goods. Sotheby's puts it as follows:

> You represent and warrant to us and the purchaser that you have the right to consign the Property for sale; that it is now, and through and including the sale will be kept, free of all liens, claims, and encumbrances of others including, but not limited to, claims of governments or governmental agencies; that good title and right to possession will pass to the purchaser free of all liens, claims, and encumbrances. . . .
>
> You agree to indemnify and hold us and the purchaser harmless from and against any claims, actions, damages, losses, liabilities, and expenses (including reasonable attorney's fees) relating to the breach or alleged breach of any of your agreements, representations, or warranties in this Agreement.

Generally, the consignment agreement does not require the consignor to make express or implied warranties regarding authenticity, condition/grade, or rarity. Consignors usually are not dealers, nor are they expected to be experts or to guarantee anything about their property. In fact, one reason collectors place property at auction is to have it examined and catalogued by the auction house's experts. As we will see in the next chapter, however, the auction house usually disclaims any legal responsibility for the correctness of catalogue descriptions. In the event of a dispute with a successful bidder, the auction house may simply rescind the sale and return disputed items to the consignor, in effect requiring the consignor to back up the auction house's own representations about the property.

Estimates

The auction house is responsible for assigning estimates to each item. Art and most collectibles auction catalogues ordinarily include estimates, but U.S. rare coin auction catalogues often do not. Catalogue estimates are the auction house's good faith prediction of the selling price of the item. That being said, however, the auction house will usually err on the low side when making estimates, in order to stimulate mail bidding. Remember that mail bidders who do not view the lots prior to the sale rely entirely on the catalogue, and the higher the estimate, the fewer mail bidders will take a chance and bid. In 1996, Sotheby's auctioned property from the estate of Jacqueline Onassis, with items selling for many times the printed estimate. A footstool once used by Caroline Kennedy was estimated by Sotheby's at $100 to $150, and it hammered down for $29,000. A rocking chair belonging to President Kennedy was estimated at $3,000 and sold for $475,000.

Sotheby's extremely low estimates served three purposes. First, they reflected Sotheby's opinion—albeit disingenuous in this case—regarding the intrinsic value of each item, without the "Jackie" provenance. Second, they helped encourage over 70,000 people to submit mail bids in the hope of acquiring something. Undoubtedly, there were many bidders on the rocking chair who would not have bothered had the estimate been in the $400,000 to $500,000 range. These bidders increased the national interest in what Sotheby's was doing, and they might bid in subsequent Sotheby's sales. Third, the low estimates made Sotheby's appear, at least to some, as having achieved miraculous results through their auctioneering skill. Auctioneers often promote themselves with examples of items selling at many times their estimates. Under the circumstances, and with due respect to Sotheby's, the results of the Onassis sale speak as much for the excitement of the buying public as for Sotheby's ability to outperform their estimates.

Estimates should be carefully reviewed with the auction house. In many cases, the auction house will agree to the estimates before the consignment agreement has even been executed, and consignors should keep a record of those discussions lest the auction house attempt to lower estimates after the deal is done.

Reserves

Estimates are very powerful tools in the auction business. However, in volatile markets such as art and collectibles, auction houses can be wrong in estimating value, and a consignor cannot assume that an item will sell above the low estimate. If bidders are absent from the sale, worried about market trends, short on cash, or just not interested in that item on that particular day, the lot will sell for the highest bid, however low that may be. In order to protect bidders from a bad market (or bad luck), auction houses allow consignors to establish reserve prices.

Reserves are confidential prices below which the lot cannot sell. They are set by the consignor, with input from the auction house, and the auction house prepares a written list of them with a copy for the consignor. Auction houses like to see reserves set no higher than 80 percent of the published estimate. At the auction, the auction house will open bidding and will bid up to the reserve price (against the other mail and floor bidders) on behalf of the consignor. If other bidders do not outbid the reserve, the lot will be "bought in" and returned to the consignor.

For consignments containing many lots, reserving each lot individually can be an imperfect protection to consignors. Some lots might sell for less than their reserves, while others sell for many times the reserve. For consignors who merely want to assure themselves an *overall* minimum price, auction houses have increasingly been offering what is called a "floating reserve." Floating reserves allow the auction house to shift reserves from one lot to another. When bidding on one item is brisk the reserve is increased, and for other lots it is lowered correspondingly. The end result is that everything sells, and the consignor receives more than the minimum amount had the same total reserve been allocated differently.

Obviously, consignors do not consign property with the intent to buy them back. However, "buy-ins" are even more unhappy events for the auction house. The auction house has done all its cataloguing, advertising, and auctioneering, but without a sale it is deprived of a seller's commission as well as a buyer's premium. Therefore, auction houses usually require some compensation in the event that a consignor buys in his own property. That "buyback fee" is usually in the area of five percent of the reserve price. If the consignor actually bids on his or her property above the reserve price, most auction houses will treat the consignor as an ordinary buyer and charge the full buyer's fee (in New York, a consignor may not bid from the floor over the reserve, although he or she is free to do so as a mail or telephone bidder).

Under New York law, the high estimate for an item cannot be lower than the reserve price. This would effectively kill the chances of a mail bidder (who will usually bid at or below the high estimate) buying an item, and even floor bidders might be so influenced by the high estimate as to bid below the price at which the auction house is permitted to sell. This rule, which accords with long-standing policy at major auction houses, was imposed in part as a result of *Cristallina v. Christie's*, 117 A.D.2d 284 (1st Dep't 1986), a case involving a group of investors who consigned to Christie's and some of whose property did not sell after having been reserved at prices substantially higher than Christie's published high estimates.

Guaranteed Minimum Prices

In larger consignments, auction houses sometimes guarantee that a certain sum will be realized by the consignor. This is different from a reserve, where failure to meet the consignor's expectations results in return of the property and a small fee to the auction house. With a guaranteed minimum price the property is allowed to sell, but if the total sales proceeds, after commissions, are less than the guaranteed amount, the auction house itself makes up the difference. In volatile markets, a consignor might want to know for certain what the consignment will bring months in the future. In addition, if the consignor is an estate or other fiduciary, guarantees eliminate the risk of market decline or some extraordinary event that dampens bidding at the auction.

Most major auction houses offer guarantees when competing for larger consignments, and some offer them to attract smaller lots as well. Consignors like to see auction houses put their own money where their estimates are. However, consignors do not always benefit from guarantees, and security has its price—auction houses usually adjust their commissions upward where there is a guarantee. Moreover, it simply is not true that whichever auction house guarantees the most money will do the best job. Finally, guarantees and reserves are somewhat incompatible, because an auction house cannot be expected to meet a guaranteed amount if high consignor reserves result in many lots failing to sell. Therefore, consignors wanting the security of reserve prices on all lots may either have to give in on guarantees or allow the auction house to control setting reserves.

Settlement—Timing and Procedure

In the auction business, payment of consignors—and return of unsold property—after the sale is called "settlement." The timing of settlement varies, but certain specific time periods tend to be used by the major auction houses. For example, Sotheby's and Christie's settle art and collectibles auctions 35 days after the date of sale, in accordance with New York's auctioneer regulations. In the rare coin field, 45 days is standard.

Settlement dates allow auction houses a certain amount of "float." As noted in Chapter 9, buyers must pay in full before taking delivery, and this usually happens promptly after a sale, particularly when the buyer is a dealer who plans on reselling the item. The auction house then has use of the funds for the remainder of the settlement period, without paying the consignor any interest. Expectations of prompt payment by buyers sometimes allows auction houses to commit to quicker settlement to a consignor in order to obtain a major consignment. I have seen auction houses offer to pay major consignors on the day of the auction, or even to deposit funds in an interest-bearing account in the consignor's name prior to the auction. Ordinarily, however, the time value of money during the settlement period is part of the auction house's compensation.

Risk of Non-Payment by the Buyer

Despite the fact that most auction buyers pay quickly, *non-payment* by the buyer is still a real risk for the consignor, particularly in volatile markets. For example, in April 1980 a major rare coin auction house faced defaults by numerous highly leveraged buyers who did not survive the steep drop in coin prices that month. Similar defaults occurred a decade later at art auctions. If the buyer simply does not show up to claim the goods, the auction house will usually "roll over" the items to its next regularly scheduled sale, arrange a private treaty sale (perhaps to one of the underbidders), or return the item to the consignor.

It is, of course, possible for the consignor to sue the buyer for breach of contract, and in cases where the market has fallen since the auction it may be beneficial to do so, because the price bid at the auction will be greater than the fair market value of the item later on. Most consignors are surprised to learn, however, that the auction house is not responsible in non-payment situations even when it delivers goods on credit to buyers who end up not paying for them. But this is generally the case in auction contracts. As in the case of an insurance loss, the auction house "assigns" its right to payment to the consignor, meaning that the consignor must make his claim directly against the delinquent buyer. In Chapter 9 we will discuss auction house credit arrangements. In collectibles auctions particularly, auction houses entice dealers to bid with 30-day credit terms. Consignors would ordinarily be indifferent to such credit policies, expecting that they will get paid regardless of whether the successful buyer pays the auction house. But when shopping around a major consignment, make sure to confirm what credit arrangements will be available and whether the auction house will protect the consignor against defaults by buying the items itself should the situation arise.

Summary

Keep the following in mind when considering a possible auction consignment:

- each area of art and collectibles has its own specialized auction houses, which can bring better results than "jacks of all trades"
- speak to more than one auction company and have them send you sample consignment agreements and terms of sale
- after you have discussed your property with each firm, get a written proposal from each
- be sure that the auction house explains the timing of the auction, its seller's and buyer's commissions, and any additional charges to you in connection with the consignment
- understand how your property will be described and estimated, and how reserves should be set
- ask how the auction house will advertise and market your property
- if your consignment is substantial, nearly everything in the consignment agreement is negotiable.

9

Buying at Public Auction

Buying at a public auction is regulated by the "terms and conditions of sale," a series of rules and regulations set forth in the auction catalogue (usually at the beginning of it), and occasionally supplemented at the commencement of the auction itself. This chapter will review the basic terms and conditions used by auction houses.

Floor Bidding

Bidders who are physically present in the sales room during the auction are called "floor bidders." The popular image of bidders raising their paddles (or twitching their noses) to be recognized by the auctioneer stems from the traditional floor bidding situation. Technology has expanded the concept of the sales "room," however. For example, Butterfield & Butterfield holds simulcasts of its auctions in Los Angeles and San Francisco, allowing floor bidders to bid to live auctioneers in two rooms—in two cities—simultaneously. Over time, these simulcast auctions may reach more distant locations. In the meantime, there are other ways that bidders may participate in the live auction without taking the time and expense of attending in person. Most major auction houses permit bidders to bid by telephone. Doing so requires a bidder to maintain a live telephone connection with the auction sales room, speaking with a member of the auction house staff who relays the bids on particular items to the auctioneer. Such bidders are, in effect, bidding from the floor, because they have complete control over whether to bid and how much to bid, just as though they were in the room physically.

Floor bidding also includes those who are represented on the floor by agents. This is a common practice at art and collectibles auctions, and dealers often represent their collector clients for a commission. Bidding through an agent saves the collector the costs of attending an auction that the dealer-agent would be attending anyway. It also enables the collector to employ the dealer's expertise to avoid purchasing the wrong items or overpaying. The commission is sometimes a small price to pay for this kind of "on the spot" back-up. However, unlike the telephone bidder, bidders who employ agents are giving up a certain amount of control over the bidding process. A prudent bidder will set dollar limits on how much the agent can bid, but within those parameters the bidder is trusting the agent to make the right decision with respect to his or her money. He or she is not there when the lot is opened for bids and can't amend the agent's instructions.

New York's auctioneer regulations (discussed in detail later in this chapter) prohibit consignors from bidding over their reserves from the floor. Presumably this is intended to discourage consignors from "bidding up" others on the floor who don't realize that their rival for a particular item is actually the item's owner.

Mail Bidding

Most bidders cannot physically attend auctions, however, and bid by mail. Mail bidding is encouraged by auction houses, both to give out-of-towners the ability to buy items as well as to create more competition for floor bidders and thereby increase the prices realized. Mail bidders receive the auction catalog and rely on the lot descriptions in the catalog or on physical inspection of lots during viewing, or both. Their bids are recorded by auction house staff who then announce them at the sale as though the bidder were there.

Mail bidding, at first blush, seems quite risky, in that the bidder has nothing but the auctioneer's estimates and his or her own value information on which to base his or her bids. Many people think that if they bid $10,000 for an item that's how much they will pay, even if the highest other bid is $1,000. This is untrue. Most auction houses would award the mail bidder the lot for the next increment over $1,000.

Another myth about mail bidding is that sales are final. As we will see below, in many cases a mail bidder who has not inspected the lot he or she purchased has greater rights than would a floor bidder.

Bidder Registration/Credit Arrangements

To bid at an auction, a buyer must be registered with the auction house. This consists of filling out a form and receiving a bidder number (printed on a "paddle" for floor bidders). Auction houses will require certain information from bidders, including name, address, and telephone number, and they may in some cases ask for a Social Security Number or driver's license information.

Where a bidder expects to bid large sums and he is unknown to the auction house, it makes sense to advise the auctioneer in advance and be approved for credit. I did this early in my career before bidding $250,000 on a rare coin on behalf of a client at a New York auction. Auction houses reserve the right to reject any bid made from the floor, and all the major auction houses have stories of people bidding huge amounts for works of art and turning out to be penniless. However, even persons well known to the auction house can default on their purchases which, as discussed in the previous chapter, can affect settlement to the consignor.

Warranty of Title

Auction houses do not make many warranties to buyers. This makes sense, because (normally) the auction house does not own the items it sells and is not, strictly speaking, the "seller." However, auction houses act as agent for the seller—the consignor. Bidders at auction do not know the consignor and cannot negotiate directly what warranties accompany the goods. Moreover, an auction house's commissions, including the buyer's premium, are in part a recognition of its expertise in authenticating and appraising the items it sells. Every day, items which might have sold for less elsewhere benefit from the increased confidence buyers have in purchasing from a major auction house. It is fair to say that auction buyers have certain expectations about items they purchase at one of the "majors." Expectations, however, do not always translate into legal rights. The UCC, which provides so many protections to ordinary retail buyers, does not apply to auction sales. Instead, what rights auction buyers have are set forth in the terms and conditions of sale prepared by the auction house and set forth in the auction catalogue.

Buyers at auction nearly always receive a warranty of title, and that is required in certain states (such as New York). We've seen in the previous chapter that auction houses require consignors to give them a warranty of title, and to indemnify and hold harmless the auction house in the event that the consignor's title to an item is challenged by someone else. The consignor's warranty and hold harmless agreement enables the auction house, in turn, to warrant title to the buyer. In some instances, such as sales of art or collectibles seized by the IRS for non-payment of taxes, even that warranty is not given, because peculiar IRS regulations permit delinquent taxpayers to pay the outstanding taxes and reclaim their property until the very moment that the successful bidder pays for it after the auction. This, of course, sometimes chills the bidding at such sales.

Disclaimer of Other Warranties

Beyond the warranty of title, there is little else that an auction house legally stands behind. Despite the extensive catalogue descriptions, and an auction house's centuries-old history, reading the terms and conditions of sale is a lesson in how to disclaim just about all responsibility to buyers in a sale of art or collectibles. Here is a typical disclaimer from a Sotheby's "Conditions of Sale" for an art auction:

> Goods auctioned are often of some age. The authenticity of the Authorship of property listed in the catalogue is guaranteed as stated in the Terms of Guarantee and except for the Limited Warranty contained therein, all property is sold "AS IS" without any representations or warranties by us or the Consignor as to merchantability, fitness for a particular purpose, the correctness of the catalogue or other description of the physical condition, size, quality, rarity, importance, medium, provenance, exhibitions, literature or historic relevance of any property and no statement anywhere, whether oral or written, whether made in the catalogue, an advertisement, a bill of sale, a salesroom posting or announcement, or elsewhere, shall be deemed such a warranty, representation or assumption of liability. . . .
>
> **Definition of Authorship.** "Authorship" is defined as the creator, period, culture, source of origin, as the case may be, as set forth in the BOLD TYPE HEADING of a lot in the catalogue, as amended by any oral or written salesroom notices or announcements. . . .
>
> **Guarantee Coverage.** Subject to the exclusions . . . below, Sotheby's warrants the Authorship (as defined above) of a lot for a period of five years from the date of sale of such lot and only to the original purchaser of record at the auction. If it is determined to Sotheby's satisfaction that the BOLD TYPE HEADING is incorrect, the sale will be rescinded. . . .
>
> **Sole Remedy.** It is specifically understood and agreed that the rescission of a sale and the refund of the original purchase price paid (the successful bid price, plus the buyer's premium) is exclusive and in lieu of any other remedy which might otherwise be available as a matter of

law, or in equity. Sotheby's and the Consignor shall not be liable for any incidental or consequential damages incurred or claimed.

Exclusions. This warranty does not apply to: (i) Authorship of any paintings, drawings or sculpture created prior to 1870, unless the lot is determined to be a counterfeit (a modern forgery intended to deceive) which has a value at the date of the claim for rescission which is materially less than the purchase price paid for the lot; or (ii) any catalogue description where it was specifically mentioned that there is a conflict of expert opinion on the Authorship of a lot; or (iii) Authorship which on the date of sale was in accordance with the then generally accepted opinion of scholars and experts; or (iv) the identification of periods or dates of execution which may be proven inaccurate by means of scientific processes not generally accepted for use until after publication of the catalogue, or which were unreasonably expensive or impractical to use.

Limited Warranty. As stated in . . . the Conditions of Sale, neither Sotheby's nor the Consignor makes any express or implied representations or warranties whatsoever concerning any property in the catalogue, including without limitation, any warranty of merchantability or fitness for a particular purpose, except as specifically provided herein.

The disclaimers of Christie's and the other major auction houses are essentially identical.

We have seen how the UCC protects retail buyers from problems relating to authenticity. Sotheby's disclaims that warranty for older works. Even with newer works, however, the terms of Sotheby's disclaimer protect Sotheby's and its consignors from the types of claims that we have discussed with retailers. Recall the Mary Cassatt painting that Sotheby's sold in 1987 (discussed in Chapter 3). After a Cassatt authentication committee was created in 1990, it declared the work a forgery, and when the buyer approached Sotheby's in 1993 to sell the painting as part of a larger consignment, Sotheby's was reluctant to do so in light of the cloud on authenticity. The buyer sued, and Sotheby's refused to refund the buyer's original $632,500 purchase price on the basis of the five-year limitation period. The parties reached an amicable settlement in early 1996 (the terms of which weren't disclosed).

An even more startling example of the auction buyer's quandary is the case of a collector who bought a Fabergé egg at a Christie's sale. Concerned that the egg was not genuine, he claimed a right of return and refused to pay Christie's. Christie's, assuring him of the egg's genuineness, sued to collect the hammer price and buyer's fee, and arranged for a written statement from a renowned Fabergé egg expert that the egg was genuine. The collector agreed to pay for the egg, as well as for Christie's legal fees. After having the egg in his safe deposit box for a few years, the collector consigned it to Christie's for sale. Christie's refused to accept the egg, doubting its genuineness. The same expert who had earlier said the egg was genuine now said he was not sure. The collector sued Christie's, and the case was eventually settled.

And a collector who bought an 1848 painting attributed to George Inness in a 1987 Sotheby's sale, and who learned authoritatively in 1995 that the painting was not by Inness, blamed Sotheby's and picketed in front of Sotheby's New York offices, attracting media attention but, as of this writing, no relief.

In rare coin and stamp sales, buyers may return lots which are counterfeit. Shreve's Philatelic Galleries, Inc., of Dallas and New York, in its terms and conditions of sale for rare stamp auctions, provides the following remedy for buyers concerned with authenticity:

> All the lots are sold as genuine. For the purpose of this sale, "genuine" is defined as not faked or forged. The following conditions apply to request for expertization: (a) Mail bidders are asked to advise of any extension requests at the time of placing their bids. (b) Floor bidders must advise of any extensions in writing at the time of lot settlement. (c) Shreves will submit all items so requested by successful bidders to the reputable authority of their choice, either the American First Day Cover Society, the American Philatelic Society or the Philatelic Foundation.

(d) Purchasers of items submitted for expertization must pay as part of the purchase price all charges for expertization, including postage and handling. (e) Purchasers of items to be expertized must make payment in full immediately upon purchase prior to expertizing. Refunds will be made promptly for all sums if in the unlikely event an item is returned with a negative opinion. Plus the buyer will be paid interest on the sums refunded at the rate of 4% per annum.

There is, of course, no ideal way to apportion the authenticity risk in auction situations between consignor, auction house, and buyer, so the approach of the major auction houses is as good as any. As a buyer, make sure you understand where the risk lies with your purchases.

With respect to grading or quality issues, the typical auction house terms and conditions provide even fewer rights. For example, in art auctions returns are only allowed in the case of items acknowledged to be counterfeit. In rare coin and stamp auctions, mail bidders may return lots for reasons of quality within a short time after receipt, generally three to five days. Even this right is sometimes lost with items carrying third-party certificates (the presumption being that mail bidders cannot disagree with the grades of certified coins or stamps), and usually there are no rights of return for floor bidders, who are assumed to have inspected the lots before bidding.

Payment Terms

Generally speaking, successful bidders at public auction must claim their items promptly and make payment. Auction houses do not extend credit to individuals, except to the extent that they accept a personal check for payment. Bidders expecting to pay substantial amounts at an auction should contact the auction house in advance to discuss payment arrangements.

Perils of Floor Bidding

The basics of bidding at auction are easy to understand, but there are certain subtle ways in which an unwary bidder might be manipulated by others in the room into overpaying for particular items. It's a good idea for less-experienced collectors and investors to use the catalog estimates as a guide, and to enter the auction with a fixed dollar limit on each and every item on which they plan to bid.

The atmosphere in an auction room can sometimes be quite feverish, and it is easy to spend more than planned, even without outside help. But consignors to auctions sometimes take advantage of inexperienced persons by bidding on their own property. Without knowing that the competing bidder is the consignor, a bidder might take such bids as validation of his or her view of the item's value, thus resulting in even higher bids. Of course, the consignor will not be the high bidder in such situations, but the bids will increase what the unwary buyer has to pay. New York City's auction regulations prohibit floor bidding by consignors, but the practice is not illegal in any other state or city. Even in New York, the consignor can submit a mail bid for his or her own property at auction.

Pooling

Bid rigging, or "pooling," consists of collusion between bidders at auction which lessens competition otherwise to be expected between them. While its most significant public impact is with the sale of public contracts, the government and private parties have brought actions to restrain and/or penalize bid rigging in a number of private contexts as well, including art and collectibles auctions.

Pooling can be attractive to buyers who don't understand that it is illegal. For example, if three similar items are being offered at an antiquities auction and three bidders are interested, it would make sense for the three to agree that only one of them will bid on each item. Each gets what he wants without having to bid against the others. Of course, from the government's standpoint, the result is an artificially low hammer price. Not only is pooling a violation of the Sherman Antitrust Act of 1890, it is a "per se" violation, meaning that once a pooling agreement has been found, the government does not have to show that prices were actually affected by the pooling. In other words, in my example above, it would not be a defense that the presence of other buyers at the auction caused the three items to sell for their fair market value anyway.

In *United States v. Ronald Pook*, Crim. No. 87-274, 1988 U.S. Dist. LEXIS 3398 (E.D. Pa. 4/18/88), antique dealers were prosecuted for pooling at antique auctions. The court noted that the Sherman Act had never been applied to antique auctions, but that "the same rules against agreements to restrain price competition apply to all economic areas." The court stated that "Consignors and auctioneers were invariably deprived by members of the pool of their proper share of the ultimate sales prices of items purchased at public auctions and sold later at private auctions." Defendants' convictions were affirmed on appeal. More recently, the Department of Justice Antitrust Division announced guilty pleas in a case involving pooling at two auctions of rare bank notes at Christie's in New York.

New York's Auction Regulations

Many states and cities impose some sort of license requirement upon auctioneers for the protection of the public who buy at auction, but only New York City, where the vast majority of art and collectibles (by dollar volume) are auctioned, regulates the auction process itself. New York's regulations are administered by the Department of Consumer Affairs and are available to the public. Their purpose is, with one exception, to protect people who buy at auction, and therefore it applies more to the terms and conditions of sale discussed in this chapter than to consignment agreements.

The regulations are, basically, disclosure requirements. Auction houses are supposed to disclose, among other things, whether they have an interest in certain items, whether they have loaned money to consignors or buyers, that there are reserves on certain items, that the auction house may bid for its own account or permit consignors to do so. Either each affected lot has a statement in its catalogue description (*e.g.*, "this lot is owned by the auction house"), or the lot description includes a symbol which, when translated, amounts to the same disclosure. Some auction houses say in so many words "some lots may be owned by the auction house and this statement is deemed to be in every lot description," which probably isn't enough.

Not all auctions are subject to the Auction Regulations. Specifically, the regulations relating to disclosure of auction house interest and the consignor's buyback rights do not apply when a written catalogue containing precise, detailed lot descriptions is available for a reasonable period of time prior to the auction, the values of lots can be determined using standard recognized reference sources, and sales are not final until the buyer has a chance to verify that the lot was as it was described. All those characteristics apply to auctions by the major art and collectibles auctioneers. Where every lot in a sale or portion of a sale is reserved, you may see a simple statement on the title page for that portion so stating. It is not sufficient to generalize in the terms and conditions that "some items might carry reserves." Sotheby's uses a ■ to mark reserved items, and Christie's uses a ● symbol before each lot number to signify that the lot carries a reserve.

New York prohibits certain auction house practices that have caused problems in the past, unless the right to do so is specifically disclosed in the terms and conditions. Among these are loaning money to bidders, using inside information to bid on items for the auction house's own account, and making consecutive bids up to the reserve price. I'm not happy with these practices anyway, and most reputable auction houses do not practice them. The only unusual requirement is that a consignor can't bid from the floor over his own reserve price, although he can bid by mail or by phone. Usually, the problem of consignors bidding up their own property is addressed by the auctioneer announcing that the consignor is bidding, but in New York there is an outright prohibition.

Part Three:
Dispute Resolution in Art and
Collectibles Transactions

10

Negotiation, Arbitration, and Litigation

My experience has been that most art and collectibles dealers and auctioneers want satisfied customers and will try to resolve problems promptly. This chapter explains some methods for dispute resolution that are used in this area and where to go if all else fails.

Negotiation—Working It Out with the Dealer

If you think you have a problem with an art and collectibles purchase, do not involve an attorney, the Better Business Bureau, or the media until you have approached the dealer or auctioneer who sold you the item and discussed the problem. This sounds so obvious, but many collectors and investors who feel that they have been cheated will either refuse to talk to someone they believe is dishonest, or will assume that the seller will not want to help them. But most art and collectibles dealers are ethical, and they also want a long-term relationship with their customers. Even those whose practices are not consistently ethical want to avoid trouble and will work with a customer who seems to know his or her rights. So the very first thing I ask someone who approaches me about a problem purchase is whether he or she has discussed the problem with the dealer or auction house.

Start the process by assembling your evidence. If the problem relates to authenticity, be prepared to explain why you believe the item to be suspect. If you believe the item was overpriced, collect relevant price information, and so on. Do your research. Arrange to share this information with the dealer, and ask the dealer to show you his or her back-up for the representations made about the item. In appropriate cases, you may wish to retain an expert to review the evidence, either on your own or in conjunction with the dealer (see "Arbitration," below). Just remember Chapters 2 and 3—the dealer owes you certain warranties, and for at least four years (the UCC statute of limitations), the dealer must be prepared to prove that the warranties were met.

The next thing to remember is not to expect a dealer to immediately rescind the purchase and refund your purchase price. Depending upon the item, rescission can be extremely burdensome to a dealer. An art gallery which is no longer showing a particular artist does not want to buy back one of that artist's works. Even dealers in more liquid items such as rare coins do not want to lose the profit on the initial sale, and if the market value of the item has fallen since the original purchase, a buyback can result in a substantial loss. Remember also that dealers and auctioneers may protect themselves through disclaimers of warranties in the purchase contracts or terms and conditions of sale. So full refunds are rarely encountered unless the amount is insubstantial, the dealer agrees that the item is fake or was misdescribed, or you make a particularly compelling case and the dealer does not want to fight with you about it. The dealer may, however, offer to buy the item back at the "wholesale" price the dealer would normally pay for the item. Or the dealer may agree to accept the item for consignment, to be sold to another customer on your behalf. Generally, should you choose to sell directly to the dealer, you may get slightly more than wholesale because the dealer wants you to be totally satisfied, and dealers and auction houses often waive commissions for consignment sales by unhappy customers.

I should note that after conferring with the dealer, you may decide that you are not entitled to a refund after all. Many investors complain when the market value of their purchase declines, but few are entitled to a refund solely because of that. Likewise, collectors who become disenchanted with a particular artist will demand their money back as though the dealer gave a lifetime buyback guarantee. Some do give such guarantees—most don't. Art and collectible items are rich with subjective descriptions, as well as associations which derive from the *buyer* and were not part of the *seller's* warranties. These are situations in which dealers simply do not have legal (or moral) obligations to their customers. And a certain degree of personal responsibility attaches to major purchases, too. I have spent much of my career representing both dealers and individual investors, and I have found that where each approaches the other in good faith and with a desire to resolve a problem, most of the time there is no need for anyone else's intervention.

Arbitration

If the dealer will not recognize your problem, or you believe that the dealer's offer is unreasonably low, you should suggest that the dispute be arbitrated. Arbitration is a very effective remedy in art and collectibles cases for several reasons. First, it is fast, with most simple cases reaching an award (ready to be confirmed as a court judgment) in a matter of weeks or, at most, months. Litigation is far slower, and often you are hostage to court backlogs and attorney schedules. Second, arbitration panels can include experts in particular fields, so that disputed matters of authenticity and market value can be heard by knowledgeable persons rather than lay judges or jurors. Third, in practically every case arbitration is far less expensive than litigation. Fourth, it is final, with the loser having virtually no chance of successfully appealing an award (and thereby delaying its implementation).

The American Arbitration Association handles arbitration cases through regional offices across the country, and among its list of available arbitrators are people from the art community. If you want to ensure in advance that disputes will be arbitrated you may place words such as the following in the contract:

> Any controversy or claim arising out of or relating to this transaction shall be settled by arbitration in accordance with the Commercial Arbitration Rules of the American Arbitration Association conducted in [city, state]. Judgment upon the award rendered by the Arbitrator may be entered in any court having jurisdiction thereof.

If there is no written contract, or if the contract does not provide for arbitration, the parties can nevertheless agree to AAA arbitration once their dispute has arisen. The AAA has submission forms which both parties sign in order to accept arbitration of their dispute.

If rare coins are involved, check to see if the dealer belongs to the Professional Numismatists Guild (PNG). PNG members must agree to arbitrate their disputes with customers through PNG. Other organizations in art and collectibles fields have similar requirements. When doing business with one of these dealers, you know that you have the option to arbitrate.

Arbitrations generally are before a sole arbitrator or panel of three arbitrators. In some cases, the parties can agree on a particular person to act as sole arbitrator and will accept his or her determination as final. In other cases, the parties will each appoint an arbitrator and the two party-appointed arbitrators will appoint the third, or "umpire." AAA provides lists of available arbitrators in specialized fields, and in the case of PNG the arbitrators are appointed by PNG itself from among its membership. Arbitrations are informal, in the sense that they are conducted in offices rather than courtrooms and lack many of the rules and procedures which encumber litigation. For example, rules of evidence are somewhat relaxed, and arbitrators are more likely to accept hearsay or unauthenticated documentary evidence than would a court. With experts as arbitrators, it is also unnecessary to educate the arbitrators about the type of item that is at issue. This means that the arbitrators can get to the point and not spend time getting up to speed.

In my experience, the results of arbitrations are at least as fair to both sides as those in litigations, and investors or collectors need not be concerned that dealer-arbitrators will be biased in favor of their fellow dealers. Dealers who serve as arbitrators generally have the highest ethical standards, and they also have a long-term view of their industries which includes a desire that disputes be fairly handled. As PNG's general counsel, I have observed rare coin arbitrations for several years, and they are extremely fair.

Litigation

Arbitration is fine for most disputes. However, if a dispute involves a great deal of money, or if it is likely to involve investigation of facts and/or complex legal issues, it may be safer to go through the court process. Judges can order recalcitrant parties to produce documents and witnesses, and while the "relaxed" attitude of arbitration is sometimes just what the parties need, in some cases firm principles must be applied to one or both sides in order to achieve justice swiftly and fairly. Moreover, arbitration is not available if both parties don't agree to it. In cases where dealer or customer or both refuse to arbitrate, litigation may be the only choice.

I always advise collectors or investors to move quickly once they determine that a negotiated or arbitrated settlement is impossible. Dealers who do not deliver goods that they sell, or who overprice investment items or falsely represent their authenticity, quality, or grade, usually do not stay in business very long. Such dealers generally attract many unhappy customers and creditors, and they are faced with a number of lawsuits in different federal and state courts around the country. Some even end up in bankruptcy or as defendants in government enforcement proceedings. It is unfortunate, but in most cases the customers who strike first get the best treatment from the legal system.

As with the purchase of art and collectibles, litigation is a business transaction that should be carefully studied. Before filing suit, you and your attorney must be on the same page regarding fees and costs. You should demand an estimate, including how much will be due from you at various stages along the way. Retainers should be carefully explained, particularly as to whether any or all of them are nonrefundable in the event that the case settles or you decide to switch attorneys. Any contingent fee agreement should be in writing and should provide for who pays out-of-pocket expenses such as travel costs, expert witness and stenographer fees. There is simply no substitute for hiring an attorney with knowledge of art and collectibles. This is an expertise that takes years to develop, and by hiring such an attorney, you will have all the benefits of that expertise and experience. Competent attorneys from outside the field have to spend a great deal of time familiarizing themselves with its unique business practices and legal rules, and even if they learn everything they need to know for the case, this knowledge will come at a high price to you.

Do not expect quick results from litigation. Court congestion and attorney schedules often create frustrating delays. Moreover, defendants often find ways of slowing down even the most determined plaintiff's team. And the process of discovering information from one another, through document requests, interrogatories, and depositions, nearly always will take months, if not years. It helps greatly if a plaintiff is focused, does his or her homework, and interacts intelligently with the attorney about the material facts and his or her litigation objectives. That way, unnecessary attorney work and expense are limited, and the issues in the case are narrowed.

Finally, be prepared to discuss settlement throughout the litigation process. Don't fight lawsuits "on principle." These types of principles can be very expensive, and we all have better things to do with our time and energy (even we attorneys!). Litigation can provide the pressure needed to move parties to settle. And judges, looking to remove one case from their workload, will often add more pressure on the parties. Sometimes it is the defendant that moves, sometimes the plaintiff, usually both. The vast majority of commercial lawsuits settle before trial. By never losing sight of the "value" of your case, you can get what you want with the least possible pain and delay.

Remedies

Whether negotiating, arbitrating, or litigating, it is important to know what remedies are available against dealers in art and collectibles cases. The available remedies depend, in large part, on the type of unlawful conduct the plaintiff is asserting and the statute or legal rule upon which the claim is based.

Breach of Contract—Rescission

One category of claims is breach of contract, which includes breach of warranty. Contract remedies generally seek to place the aggrieved plaintiff where he or she would have been had there been no breach. For the types of breaches described in Chapters 2 and 3, *i.e.*, sale of unauthentic or improperly described art or collectible items, the most common remedy is rescission. Rescission is reversal of the contract—return of the goods in exchange for refund of the purchase price. The dealer, having made the warranty, must suffer having the defective item back.

Even when the market value of the item has fallen since the date of purchase, the courts have said that it is not unfair to require the dealer to return the full purchase price, the assumption being that there would never have been a sale in the first place if the buyer had known the truth about the item. On the other hand, it is quite unusual in a contract or warranty case for the plaintiff to recover *more* than the contract price, such as prejudgment interest, attorney's fees, or multiple damages. And consequential damages, *i.e.*, the lost profit that would have been made had the item been as described (or had the money been invested elsewhere), usually are not awarded either.

Common Law Torts—Damages

In some cases, breach of warranty claims aren't made, either because the four-year statute of limitations has expired, or because the warranties were ambiguous and/or disclaimed. In such cases, and others where more serious wrongdoing took place, buyers claim under tort law. Torts include fraud, breach of fiduciary duty, negligence, and product liability. With art and collectibles, the most often seen tort claim is common law fraud. By asserting that the dealer knowingly deceived him or her regarding a material aspect of the purchase, the buyer makes available certain rights and remedies which do not exist in breach of warranty claims.

First, the claim can be brought more than four years after the purchase. The limits in UCC §2-725 do not apply to fraud claims, and most states' laws incorporate a "discovery rule" into their tort laws. Thus, the limitations period begins only when plaintiffs discover that they have been defrauded, or in the exercise of reasonable diligence should have discovered it.

Second, a fraud claim can be asserted by someone other than the original purchaser, provided that the dealer could reasonably have foreseen that this type of person would obtain the product. For example, the wholesale distributor of a print might prepare brochures containing representations and then sell the prints and brochures to retail galleries. If a retail buyer learns that some of the representations were false, he or she can sue the gallery for breach of warranty. But what if the gallery is out of business? While breach of warranty is only available against the gallery, a fraud claim might be made against the distributor who prepared and disseminated the brochures.

Third, proving fraud will entitle the buyer to a wider scope of damages. It is not uncommon for courts to award buyers *the greater* of rescission plus interest or the value of the item had it been described correctly. In the case of an investor in art who was fraudulently sold a fake, the court stated that rescission was not good enough because the market value of that artist's genuine works had increased dramatically since the date of purchase. The damages would be the difference in present value between the fake and the original. In addition, in fraud cases the chances of recovering consequential damages and attorney's fees are greater.

Statutory Violations—Differing Remedies

We have seen that a number of different federal and state statutes provide rights of action for buyers of art and collectibles, and there are some definite benefits to asserting claims under these statutes. The three relevant federal statutes are the Telemarketing Act, the Lanham Act, and the Hobby Protection Act, all of which were discussed in earlier chapters.

The Telemarketing Act allows individuals to bring lawsuits for unfair or deceptive practices that previously only the FTC or state attorney general could bring. Provided that the plaintiff meets the threshold of $50,000 in damages and the transaction involves interstate activity (*i.e.*, an out-of-state dealer or supplier), suit can be brought in federal court for damages, including attorney's fees. The plaintiff must notify the FTC in writing before filing suit, and the FTC has the right to intervene and take over the case, presumably if it determines that the public interest is at stake.

The Lanham Act, discussed in Chapter 7, is the federal unfair trade practices statute, authorizing suits in federal court where the origin, quality/grade, or provenance of goods is misrepresented to consumers. While the Lanham Act is often used to combat "knock-offs" of trademarked items such as Rolex watches, it is equally applicable to art or collectible items whose value depends so much on the correctness of such representations. The Lanham Act allows consumers to recover double or triple damages in cases of knowing and willful conduct by the dealer, and it also allows recovery of attorney's fees. It is a powerful tool for consumer protection.

Finally, the Hobby Protection Act, discussed in Chapter 7, allows purchasers of replica coins or political memorabilia not clearly marked as such to sue for damages and recover their attorney's fees as well.

State statutes also add to the remedies available to buyers of art and collectibles. In addition to the rights of the states themselves to bring suit (see Chapter 11), private rights of action are created in most states' consumer protection laws. The New York and California laws described in Chapters 2 and 3 provide some rights specifically in the areas of fine art prints and autographed sports memorabilia, but in other collecting areas the general consumer protection laws will also support claims. The only prerequisites for a right of action under state consumer laws are that some part of the transaction have taken place in the state and that the consumer attempted to resolve the dispute with the dealer by sending a written claim more than 30 days before filing suit.

One benefit of asserting private rights under federal or state statutes is that these rights cannot be disclaimed or waived, unlike the right to bring breach of warranty actions. For example, Texas Deceptive Trade Practices–Consumer Protection Act §17.42 essentially eliminates any inadvertent waivers by consumers, by requiring that waivers (1) be in writing and signed by the consumer; (2) that the consumer not be in a disparate bargaining position with the dealer and be represented by an attorney of his or her own choosing; (3) that the waiver be conspicuous and have a heading "Waiver of Consumer Rights"; and (4) that the waiver read essentially as follows:

> I waive my rights under the Deceptive Trade Practices–Consumer Protection Act, Section 17.41 *et seq.*, Business & Commerce Code, a law that gives consumers special rights and protections. After consultation with an attorney of my own selection, I voluntarily consent to this waiver.

So even after agreeing to a disclaimer of express and implied warranties, a buyer of art and collectibles retains his or her rights under consumer protection statutes. Another benefit is a generally longer statute of limitations, because of the "discovery rules." And perhaps most important is the ability to recover multiple damages and attorney's fees, which gives consumers greater leverage in negotiating a settlement.

11

The FTC and Other Government Agencies

Collectors and investors who believe that they have been cheated often seek the government's assistance in recovering their money and putting the bad guys out of business. In the art and collectibles world, the leading federal regulatory agency is the Federal Trade Commission. On the state level, the various attorney general's offices handle hundreds, if not thousands, of complaints relating to art and collectibles each year.

The FTC

The Federal Trade Commission is empowered, among other things, to enforce FTC Act §5, which prohibits "unfair or deceptive acts or practices in commerce." Misrepresentations of material facts made to induce the purchase of goods or services violate §5. In the 1980s, the FTC began to be interested in practices in the art and collectibles fields, particularly the sale of fine art prints and rare coins as investments. Through its Bureau of Consumer Protection in Washington, DC, the

FTC continues to investigate and prosecute dealers and others in these and other fields.

The FTC invites consumer complaints against retailers. However, the FTC does not resolve individual complaints. Rather, it looks for patterns of conduct which threaten *the public as a whole*. Therefore, the FTC typically will not commence an investigation on the basis of only one or two complaints. Those consumers will be referred to other dispute resolution mechanisms or advised to seek private remedies in court. In truly exceptional cases the FTC will, on its own initiative, investigate a company whose advertising and other practices may violate the FTC Act.

The standard the FTC applies under §5 is one of deception: Would a reasonable person of average intelligence have relied upon, and been misled by, the representations and/or omissions made by the dealer? As with fraud claims generally, the misrepresentations must be material and must cause consumer harm in the absence of market declines or other factors. The FTC's specific focus over the years has been improper marketing of speculative, high-markup items as safe, low-risk investments. An extended quotation from an opinion of the Eighth Circuit Court of Appeals in *FTC v. Security Rare Coin & Bullion Corp.*, 931 F.2d 1312 (8th Cir. 1991) shows the reasoning behind FTC prosecution of one collectibles dealer:

> Security Coin was in the business of selling rare coins, a highly technical and specialized commodity unfamiliar to most consumers. Security Coin marketed foreign and domestic coins through telephone solicitation, direct mail, and advertisements in its own financial publications and in national newspapers. Security Coin represented its coins as excellent low-risk investments sold at or near market value with superior liquidity and profit potential. Security Coin sought to overcome consumer resistance and concern about risk by heavily promoting the existence of a "buyback" policy, under which it would repurchase coins at a discount from its current sales prices. These promotions resulted in substantial sales of coins.

Security Coin graded the value of its own coins and arbitrarily marked up the price of the coins sold to consumers two or three times the wholesale price. Because the coins would have to double or triple in value before any gain could be realized, Security Coin's representations as to their investment value were fraudulent. . . .
To satisfy the reliance requirement in actions brought under . . . the Act, the FTC need merely show that the misrepresentations or omissions were of the kind usually relied upon by reasonable and prudent persons, that they were widely disseminated, and that the injured consumers actually purchased the defendants' products. Security made credible and persuasive misrepresentations concerning the coins' allegedly low prices, high profit potential, and low risk. These are key factors in a consumer's decision to purchase coins for investment purposes. We agree with the district court and the FTC that it was reasonable for consumers entering this specialized and technical market to rely on the representations of an apparently reputable firm staffed by experts and specializing in such investments.

When debating implementation of the Telemarketing Act in 1995, FTC representatives sought to require that dealers in "tangible assets" (which includes art and collectible items) disclose to customers the amount they actually paid for the items they sell, and also disclose "all material facts" before accepting any money from the customer. Although the final version of the Telemarketing Sales Rule did not contain specific regulations aimed at tangible assets dealers, the FTC showed its particular concern for this area of the investment marketplace.

The FTC has no criminal jurisdiction, but instead proceeds through civil enforcement actions in federal district court. Quite frequently, where the FTC fears dissipation of assets and wants to prevent additional consumer fraud, it will ask the court for an immediate injunction against misrepresentations, a freeze of the dealer's assets, and the appointment of a receiver to manage the dealer's business. I have served as a receiver in an FTC action, and I also have been appointed Special Counsel at the request of the FTC in another case. Ultimately, FTC complaints seek permanent injunctions against unlawful behavior as well as monetary redress to consumers who have been harmed by that behavior. As a result of FTC action, many unscrupulous art and collectibles investment firms have been shut down and their principals punished. Unfortunately, the FTC has not been particularly successful at providing monetary redress in art and collectibles cases, primarily because the principals are bankrupt and "judgment-proof" by the time the FTC gets to them. I advise many consumer clients to notify the FTC about their unsatisfactory experiences with art and collectibles dealers, but I don't recommend starting with the FTC to resolve a specific dispute or get a refund.

State Attorneys General

At the state level, attorneys general enforce state consumer protection laws, such as Massachusetts's Chapter 93A and Texas's Deceptive Trade Practice–Consumer Protection Act, Tex. Business & Commerce Law §17.41 *et seq.* These laws are sometimes referred to as "baby FTC Acts" because they usually overlap with the protections provided by §5 of the FTC Act. In addition, in states such as New York and California which have specific statutes relating to the protection of art and collectibles buyers, the attorneys general of those states are charged with protecting the public interest. Unfair or deceptive practices such as would violate the FTC Act also probably would be actionable under the state equivalents.

The trick is to get a state agency interested in your problem. If the dealer is located out of state, as is frequently the case in investment fraud cases, an attorney general's office might not want to prosecute, although this is changing with the Telemarketing Act, which authorizes state attorneys general to sue in federal court on behalf of its residents even when the defendant is elsewhere. State agencies are closer and more accessible than the FTC, and they are far more likely to intervene in particular cases involving their residents. An attorney general's consumer protection division will forward consumer complaints to the dealer involved and request a response from the dealer. Dealers that refuse to cooperate, or whose responses are unsatisfactory, may be investigated further. States have powers similar to the FTC with respect to freezing assets, enjoining unlawful conduct, and providing consumer redress.

In art market states such as New York and California, as we saw in earlier chapters, additional legislation exists specifically addressing problems in the art and collectibles businesses, and generally those laws are enforced by the state attorney general. For example, the New York attorney general can sue to get an injunction against dealer's violation of the disclosure laws for autographed sports collectibles, fine prints, and sculptures, as well as for restitution payments to injured customers, and civil penalties of $1,000 per violation ($500 in the case of fine prints or sculptures).

Finally, local agencies such as the New York Department of Consumer Affairs regulate practices in the art and collectibles fields. New York's Auction Regulations, which I touched on in Chapter 9, are issued by and enforced by that organization.

Part Four:
Tax Aspects of Art and Collectibles

12

Sales, Use, and Income Tax

There is very little we do in the United States today that is not somehow affected by the tax laws. Buying and selling art and collectibles is no exception. An understanding of basic principles of state and local sales and use tax, income tax, and estate tax will not only assure compliance with the law, but it may save you money as well. Of course, although I have tried to accurately present this complicated subject, be warned that tax laws change quite often and that differences in geography, income, and portfolio composition may change considerably the effect of taxes. You should always consult a competent attorney or tax advisor to update yourself and to tailor any tax strategies to your particular situation.

Sales Tax

Some state and local governments impose a sales tax on retailers for the privilege of retailing tangible personal property. The tax is usually a percentage of the gross sale price of the goods and is remitted by the dealer along with a sales tax return. While the dealer is actually liable for sales tax, a nearly universal practice is to pass the cost of sales taxes on to the re-

tail customer. In a typical over-the-counter sale of art and collectibles, the dealer will add the appropriate sales tax to the invoice price of the goods.

The taxable event for sales tax is an in-state retail sale. This
leads to two common exemptions to sales tax. First, sales tax is
not due on wholesale (dealer-to-dealer) sales, but only if the
buyer holds a valid resale permit or certificate from that state
or another state. Second, sales to out-of-state customers are
exempt from sales tax if (1) the customer orders goods directly
from the retailer; and (2) the goods are shipped from outside
the customer's state and no in-state branch, office, outlet, or
other place of business of the seller participates in the sale.

In certain states, some sales of rare coins are specifically
exempted from sales tax for various reasons. States which do
not apply sales tax to the sale of money exempt sales of "coins
of the realm," defined as coins which remain legal tender of
the United States or a foreign government. Others do not tax
investment purchases, and these states assume that "bulk"
purchases of over $1,000 are for investment. However, in
most states, unless the sale falls into one of the common exemptions, sales tax will apply.

Dealers occasionally ask buyers of expensive items
whether they wish goods to be shipped to a friend or relative
in a neighboring state, thereby relieving the dealer of the responsibility to charge sales tax. If the item is actually shipped,
a sales tax exemption may apply. *Never* take the item with you
and allow an empty package to be shipped out of state. If a
dealer wishes to cheat the state, you shouldn't voluntarily participate in the scheme.

Use Tax

Recently, the collectibles marketplace has seen states become
much more aggressive in enforcing their right to collect use
tax on certain sales. While sales tax is triggered by a dealer's
exercise of the privilege of doing retail business in a state, use
tax is based entirely on the purchase of property for use in the

taxing state. The taxable event is the purchase, not the sale, and the tax is due from the buyer, not the dealer. Use tax is far more difficult to predict than is sales tax. For one thing, the sale need not take place in the taxing state, provided that the buyer resides there. This means that mail order purchases which are clearly exempt from sales tax nevertheless are subject to use tax. States are quite candid in saying that use tax levels the playing field between local dealers who have to pay sales tax and their out-of-state competitors who don't. Generally, states hold dealers responsible for collecting and remitting use tax on behalf of their customers, and for all practical purposes states will not attempt to collect back taxes from individual customers if the dealer itself is solvent. However, the liability is there, and it can continue indefinitely if the unwary buyer does not file a use tax return.

The states with the largest collectibles markets, such as New York and California, are leading the way on use tax. They stipulate that dealers with an in-state office, agent, warehouse, or other permanent physical presence have a close enough "nexus" with their states to require collecting use tax on all sales to their residents. But these states have also aggressively audited dealers with no permanent physical presence there, even dealers who just attend local coin shows. For example, in July 1995, California's Board of Equalization announced that attending a single retail coin show in California might create nexus, causing the American Numismatic Association to move its 1996 early spring fair from Santa Clara to Tucson, Arizona. In June 1995, New York's highest court ruled that Orvis, a Vermont mail order seller of outdoor equipment, acquired "nexus" with New York after Orvis personnel made 12 trips to New York City over a three-year period to monitor product displays at independent stores which carry Orvis products. Orvis's personnel did not attend shows or even make a single sale in New York. Nexus guidelines prepared by the Multistate Tax Commission, an organization created by state taxing authorities, hint that even a short appearance at a coin show will trigger nexus. This area of law is likely to change in the future,

as states realize the dangers of discouraging out-of-state dealers from doing business there.

Income Tax

Net income from the sale of art and collectibles is taxable, but
not until the item is sold or otherwise disposed of for value.
For some people, this makes art and collectibles a preferred
investment vehicle over stocks, whose dividends are taxed an-
nually even if they are in the form of new stock and not cash.
An investor can defer taxable gains until a time of his or her
own choosing. However, the relative tax advantages of art and
collectibles *vis a vis* other forms of investment are beyond the
scope of this book, and I recommend specialized advice from
financial professionals in your state.

For the purposes of this discussion, the key income tax
aspects of purchases and sales of art and collectibles relate to
the treatment of expenses and losses, and they depend largely
upon whether you are a collector, an investor, or a dealer for
tax purposes. Sounds simple enough, but many people spend
a lot of time and effort arguing with the IRS and state taxing
authorities over this characterization, because the tax consequences of each can be quite different.

Collectors, who buy and sell art and collectible items primarily for personal pleasure, are the most tax-*disadvantaged*
class. They must pay tax on income they earn from their collections but cannot deduct net losses they might have. They
cannot deduct any expenses relating to their collection, such
as insurance, security, membership dues for clubs and sub-
scriptions to periodicals, but can offset these expenses against
any net income they declare from sales. Unfortunately, even
this benefit is substantially limited because it comprises a
"miscellaneous" itemized deduction on Schedule A subject to
the two percent adjusted gross income floor. In other words,
unless the collector's total miscellaneous expenses exceed two
percent of adjusted gross income, there is no benefit. Collectors are entitled to treat their collectibles as capital assets after

a one-year holding period, but the difference between tax rates for capital gains and ordinary income is not as great today as it has been in the past.

Investors fare slightly better. They can deduct expenses relating to their art and collectibles portfolios, but not net losses from sales. However, the IRS makes it more and more difficult to qualify as an investor, clearly preferring to characterize everyone interested in art and collectibles as a collector. The key is whether the taxpayer is engaged in the activity for profit or for enjoyment. Taxpayers who show a profit from their activities for three of the past five years are presumed to be engaged in those activities for profit, although the IRS has the right to rebut that presumption. Relevant factors are the amount of time the taxpayer spent on the activity, whether the taxpayer relied on advice of experts, and whether losses could be expected in a particular year (such as when the market drops in particular types of art or collectibles).

Finally, taxpayers who can establish that they buy and sell art or collectibles as part of a trade or business may acquire dealer status, enabling them to deduct expenses as well as net losses against their other income. As one might expect, the IRS is loath to treat a collector with other sources of income as a collectibles "dealer." However, over the years the regulations in this area have been expanded so that it is not impossible for a serious enthusiast to qualify. The "for profit" determination is similar to that described above for investors. Dealers pay tax at ordinary income rates and may use losses to offset other ordinary income.

One word about "wash sales." Many retailers offer tax breaks to collectors and investors whose tax basis in their portfolios is higher than their current value. The pitch is for the taxpayer to sell their portfolios to the dealer for a loss, take off the loss against capital gain income in that tax year, and then plow the proceeds of the sale back into more art or collectibles. The sale and tax loss part of the deal is fine. If the assets meet the holding period requirements, the losses can offset income. However, even by taking a small commission on the purchase, most retailers cannot afford to acquire large portfolios without a ready customer. Consequently, I regularly see dealers offering to buy rare coin, stamp, or sports-card portfolios which have declined in value, and then sell them back to the customer 30 days later at their current market price, a transaction which the IRS calls a "wash sale." Where the intent of the transaction is simply to generate a loss, the IRS will disallow that loss. Moreover, dealers who offer these deals generally take commissions on both ends, which would not be necessary were the prices fair to begin with.

Like-Kind Exchanges and Barter Transactions

A popular marketing tool for retailers of art and collectibles is the "like-kind" exchange under Section 1031 of the Internal Revenue Code. That Code provision allows investors in art and collectibles to trade items which have appreciated in value for items of the same "nature or character" without recognizing income or capital gains on the transaction. For investors interested in shifting from one area to another, this can be a good tax-avoidance technique. However, it must be carefully done to conform with the Code, and several restrictions limit the availability of the like-kind exchange.

The first limitation on like-kind exchanges involves the parties themselves. Like-kind exchanges between "related parties" such as relatives or controlled corporations or other entities will not receive 1031 treatment. Second, both the items being traded and those received must be held purely for investment purposes, necessitating the types of proofs described above to distinguish investors from collectors. Third, the items must truly be of "like-kind," and the IRS has been difficult there. For example, a trade of gold U.S. rare coins (such as a 1927 $20 gold piece) for gold U.S. bullion coins (such as a 1995 gold Eagle) will not qualify. Finally, the exchange does not eliminate the tax, but only defers it.

Barters are trades of property at their market value, without cash changing hands. Where items are clearly not "like-kind," collectors and investors nevertheless attempt to avoid income tax on appreciated value by bartering with one another. While taxable gain on art and collectible items is not recognized until the items are sold, a barter is treated by the IRS as a "sale" because the taxpayer is disposing of the item in exchange for value. The celebrated artist Peter Max was indicted in 1996 for failing to report income from the barter of nearly $1 million of artworks for the purchase of two residences.

One last point—like-kind exchanges and barters are not necessarily exempt from sales or use taxes, and if a dealer is involved it is best to check on this before completing the deal.

Art and Collectibles in IRAs

Until the Reagan 1981 tax law took effect on January 1, 1982, art and collectibles (the IRS lumps them together under the term "collectibles") could be purchased for placement in an IRA or other retirement plan. Since that date, purchase of art or collectibles by a retirement plan has been deemed a distribution for tax purposes. This change had a profound effect on the market in rare coins and other investment collectibles, as one of the primary motivations for purchase vanished, literally overnight. The IRS made it clear that if such assets were already contained in retirement accounts, they could stay there tax-free. The question remains, however, can taxpayers "roll over" art and collectibles without causing an involuntary distribution? The IRS has not given any clear answer to this question. In any event, in 1986 Congress carved out a small exception to the IRA ban with the introduction of the U.S. Mint American Eagle program. U.S. commemorative gold and silver coins dated 1986 and later may be purchased for retirement accounts. And every year, bills are introduced to expand this exception to include all U.S. legal tender coins. If you are interested, contact a tax or legal professional for the latest information.

Record-Keeping Requirements

For various reasons, anyone purchasing a sizable amount of art or collectible items should keep detailed records regarding such purchases. The prices paid for each item should be detailed as well as the date of purchase, so that if the item is sold the gain (or loss) can be calculated and characterized, *i.e.*, as capital gain or ordinary income. In addition, if the taxpayer intends to deduct any expenses relating to such items, those expenses should be paid by check and an invoice or receipt obtained. If necessary, a note should state the purpose of the expense, so that it can be proven to be within the expenses allowable by law.

Buyers of art and collectibles should realize that dealers also have documentation requirements. Most dealers record every sale, no matter how small, and issue an invoice to the buyer. For cash transactions over $10,000, dealers must file a report to the IRS on Form 8300 and send a copy to the buyer.

When selling all or part of a collection, all relevant records should be kept for at least 10 years after the sale. This enables the taxpayer to fulfill all record-keeping requirements for collectors, investors, and dealers. If possible, commissions, state and local sales tax, and other selling expenses should be itemized and in writing.

13

Estate Planning and Charitable Donations of Art and Collectibles

This is an extremely complicated area of law, and it changes slightly with every major revision of the tax code. However, for three reasons art and collectibles are uniquely difficult assets to deal with in tax planning. First, because art and collectibles can increase greatly in value over time, taxpayers often search for ways to minimize the tax impact of such appreciation when they sell or bequeath their collections. Second, because the study and display of art and collectibles is deemed to be in the public interest, tax-exempt organizations such as museums and universities actively pursue donations of such items. Third, because the values of art and collectibles are so subjective, and may differ for different purposes, there is room for serious argument between taxpayers and the IRS.

Estate Tax

Most taxpayers need not concern themselves with estate tax avoidance. Based on current (1997) estate tax thresholds, only those whose estates are likely to exceed $600,000 have any estate tax liability. Moreover, the so-called "marital deduction"—whereby collectors may remove the value of their collections from their estates by transferring title to their spouses in their wills—remains unlimited. Nevertheless, taxpayers likely to leave substantial estates upon death should work with competent professionals to develop an appropriate estate plan. *All* taxpayers possessing collections of art or collectibles should be aware of the basic rules governing their part in an estate plan.

The decedent's basis in art and collectibles will be stepped up to the fair market value at time of death. For valuable collections accumulated over time, this can result in surprises, as items for which the decedent paid relatively little are valued much higher. However, stepping up basis can be a huge benefit if proper planning is done. For example, by bequeathing art or collectibles to a spouse, the decedent allows the spouse to acquire items tax-free at fair market value. The spouse can then sell those items without recognizing any gain or income, years' worth of appreciation in value going untaxed. Most of these same benefits also accrue to taxpayers who make gifts of art and collectibles to their spouses during their lifetimes, although certain guidelines should be followed when doing this. The stepping-up is also beneficial to non-spouses who receive testamentary gifts of art or collectibles, although in those cases the assets will not be deducted from the decedent's estate. The best approach is often to take advantage both of the marital deduction and the $600,000 tax-free allowance by allocating part of the estate to the spouse and part to the decedent's children. This protects the surviving spouse from estate tax at the spouse's death, when no marital deduction can be taken.

Charitable Gifts of Art or Collectibles

Taxpayers often make lifetime or testamentary gifts of appreciated art and collectibles to charitable organizations. Indeed, many taxpayers *create* charities just to receive, manage, and distribute their collections. The intricacies of using tax-exempt organizations for philanthropic or tax-avoidance purposes is beyond this chapter or the book as a whole, and substantial IRS penalties for overvaluing charitable gifts require some care when donating art or collectibles. What follows are some basic questions when evaluating charitable donations of art or collectibles.

The first question is whether the property being given is long-term capital gain property. If it is, the charitable donor may deduct the full fair market value of the property at the time of the gift, including market appreciation. If not, the donor can deduct only his or her actual basis in the property, which is generally the amount the donor paid for the property. Generally speaking, art or collectibles held more than one year will be considered long-term capital gain property. A major exception, however, applies to artists holding their original works. Because the IRS considers an artist's own works "inventory" or "ordinary income property," artists who donate their works to charity may deduct only the value of the "paint and canvas" incorporated into the work. For collectors or investors who donate property they have held for less than one year, the deduction is also usually limited to the price they paid for the property, because the IRS considers such property short-term capital gain property.

The next question is the use to which the charity puts the donated items. Charities sometimes accept gifts for their own use as part of their regular activities, and in other cases charities sell gift items as part of their fund raising. According to the Internal Revenue Code, items of tangible personal property which the charity puts to a use "not unrelated" to the charity's tax-exempt purpose may be deducted to their full fair market value, but items which the charity uses for "unrelated" purposes may not. Here is the example given by the IRS in Publication 526, entitled "Charitable Deductions":

> If a painting contributed to an educational institution is
> used by that organization for educational purposes by

being placed in its library for display and study by art students, the use is not an unrelated use. But if the painting is sold and the proceeds are used by the organization for educational purposes, the use is an unrelated use.

The most common "unrelated use" in the art and collectibles field is the charity auction, in which collectors donate items to be sold for the benefit of charitable organizations. The IRS's example demonstrates the peculiar nature of the "related-unrelated" distinction. A collector choosing between two organizations to which to donate a particular item might well find that one organization would put the item to a related use while the other would not. If the item is one which has appreciated greatly over time, donating to the former charity might result in a much higher tax deduction.

Quite often, donors are not in a position to know how their gifts of property will be used by charities, and charities do not ordinarily know the donor's tax basis in donated property, or whether the property had been held for more than a year prior to the donation. In other words, neither donor nor charity may be aware of whether the gift will result in the maximum tax benefits to the donor. Moreover, what happens when a gift is displayed for a while in the charity's library and *then* sold? The IRS allows donors who believed in good faith that their gifts were to be used for "not unrelated" purposes to take their full fair market value deduction, even if the property is ultimately sold, but only if the charity holds the property for one year. If the charity sells a donated item within two years of acquiring it, however, the charity must file Form 8282 with the IRS giving the donor's name and the amount for which the item was sold. This enables the IRS to check the "fair market value" deduction taken by the donor against the actual value received by the charity when the item was sold.

Third, at the risk of oversimplifying a complicated area, the extent of deductions even for long-term capital gain property put to a related use by the charity depends upon whether the charity is publicly supported or is a private foundation, and whether the taxpayer wishes to deduct full fair market value in the current year or spread out ("carry over," in IRS parlance) the deduction over time, up to five years. Taxpayers may deduct gifts to public charities of up to 50 percent of the taxpayer's adjusted gross income in any given year, while donations to private charities are limited to 30 percent and, in some cases, to 20 percent. If you don't know which category a particular charity falls under, the IRS says just ask them: "You may ask any organization whether it is a 50-percent limit organization, and most will be able to tell you." But gifts of capital gain property are limited to 30 percent regardless of the recipient, unless the taxpayer elects to deduct only his or her basis and not any appreciation. Deciding which way to go depends upon the amount of appreciation in the property to be donated, the taxpayer's adjusted gross income for that year and projected into the future, and other charitable gifts which the taxpayer may be contemplating. Be sure to get expert advice here.

Valuations/Qualified Appraisals

Beyond the complexities of charitable deduction law lies the subjectivity of art and collectibles values, which create problems even when everyone agrees on the nature of the gifts or donations themselves. As we have seen, an executor of an estate will want to understate the values of art and collectibles in the taxable estate while at the same time hoping to get away with *overstating* the value of items bequeathed to a spouse. Taxpayers also want high valuations for art and collectibles they donate to charity (for their income tax deductions) and low valuations for gifts to non-spouses (to reduce or eliminate gift tax). The IRS, if it reviews the appraised values, will tend toward the opposite positions in each situation (low valuations for charitable gifts and high valuations in estate situations), and the IRS employs art and collectibles experts who often back up their positions. This is an inherent conflict that shows up quite often in evaluating estate tax returns and charitable deductions of art and collectibles.

Experts will disagree over what "market" to use in measuring fair market value, as between retail, wholesale, or auction. Substantial differences may exist between these different market levels, and taxpayers should expect the IRS to seek the prices least favorable to the taxpayer's position.

Another common issue when estates include art and collectibles is whether auction prices for comparable sales used to establish value should include the buyer's premium. This 10 to 25 percent difference can, of course, be significant. I favor including the buyer's premium because, as we have seen, auction buyers generally factor the premium into their bidding calculations.

In addition, experts debate the extent to which "blockage," *i.e.,* the loss of value associated with selling a collection as a unit, will affect appraised values for estates or large gifts. A great example of this was the estate of artist Georgia O'Keeffe, in which the IRS and the estate agreed on the total value of some 400 works she bequeathed to various charities and individuals, but were tens of millions of dollars apart on the extent to which blockage and costs of sale reduced their value for tax purposes (a court finally decided upon a 50-percent reduction).

The best way to minimize valuation problems is to employ a professional appraiser who follows guidelines set forth in IRS Publication 561, "Determining the Value of Donated Property." These guidelines require appraisals to include references to sales of comparable items, such as other works by the same artist, as well as some statement regarding the present market in the type of item being appraised. They also limit who can act as an appraiser in this context. The dealer from whom the collector purchased the item, any expert who derives 50 percent of his or her appraisal income from doing appraisals for the collector or the charity, and any family member of such persons cannot perform appraisals for tax purposes.

Acknowledgment and
Reporting Requirements

For any donation of over $250 in value, the donor must receive an acknowledgment from the charity at the time of the donation in order to take a charitable deduction on the item(s). This acknowledgment must be in writing, must be signed by an appropriate person within the charity, and must describe in reasonable detail the item being donated. The charity does not value the item and does not verify the value placed on it by the donor, so in borderline cases the donor and charity should agree that an acknowledgment is due. Note that the acknowledgment is not sent to the IRS by either the donor or the charity.

If the donation exceeds $500 in value, the donor must file IRS Form 8283 with his or her tax return. That form requires information regarding the charity, the date of the gift, a description of the property, and the donor's original cost basis in the property.

For donations above $5,000, the donor must get a written appraisal, summarize the appraisal on Form 8283, and have the charity sign the Form 8283. Again, by signing the Form 8283 the charity does not agree that the donor's valuation of the item is correct. The donor does not send the appraisal to the IRS, but only a summary.

Finally, when donating art valued at over $20,000, the written appraisal itself must be attached to IRS Form 8283 and filed with the donor's tax return.

Table of Authorities

Statutes

Regulations

Cases

Index